# STOP
# WORKING
# FOR
# UNCLE SAM

SUNDAY ADELAJA

Sunday Adelaja
**Stop Working For Uncle Sam**
©2017 Sunday Adelaja
ISBN 978-1-908040-34-3

Cover design by Alexander Bondaruk
Interior design by Olena Kotelnykova

© Sunday Adelaja, 2017,
The Mountain Of Ignorance — Milton Keynes, UK:
Golden Pen Limited, 2017

# TABLE OF CONTENTS

# INTRODUCTION

Although man throughout history has had to work to meet his needs, modern society wants people to believe they have gained economic freedom, when in actuality they are bound in servitude. Modern society is structured and characterized by a form of slavery almost unknown to a lot of people.

Modern day slavery manifests in many forms and it is largely self-inflicted. People ultimately make the choice to come under oppressive conditions in order to survive in today's consumer driven economy.

Millions of people in employment today wake up every day unhappy, unfulfilled, like drones with zero motivation, just going through the motions all in the name of survival.

It is obvious that people are selling themselves; their time, talents and sacrificing family happiness just for mere survival and an illusory sense of financial security. As you pick up this book, I want you to know that your life is too precious to end up in mediocrity. No single human being was created to just find employment, earn a salary, retire and die. Every human being is born to answer a particular cry of humanity. You too were born for something big.

Instead of putting maximum, best effort and energy into discovering, harnessing and developing the potential within and finding freedom through self-expression, unfortunately, many people are going around looking for employment. Looking for jobs that trap them for life and they can't do anything about it. They are looking for employment that robs them of a rewarding and meaningful work experience.

"Only you are responsible for your life and for making it a happy life" therefore quit blaming other people or the system and take control of your life.

Let's take a look at a bible snapshot of two brothers found in the book of Genesis.

Born from the same father and mother, two brothers with two different destinies, the story of Esau and Jacob is simply intriguing.

Isaac was a very rich and wealthy man. After much waiting, Rebecca, Isaac's wife had twins, Esau and Jacob.

The Boys grew. Esau became a cunning hunter, a wild man loving the outdoors. His brother, on the other hand, preferred the familiar surroundings; he simply kept the family flocks.

One day Jacob was cooking a local delicacy soup when Esau came running in from his hunting expedition. And he was very hungry. The aroma of the soup Jacob was preparing was simply irresistible; Esau just had to have some of that soup.

Jacob saw the desperation in Esau's eyes. Nothing else mattered at that moment to Esau but the need to fulfill his hunger.

As Jacob dillydallied, Esau shouted, "Quick, give me some of that soup".

Realizing an opportunity, Jacob asked, "What will you give me in return?"

Jacob went on with his demand and said, "How about giving me your birthright in exchange for my soup?"

The birthright was a potential of ownership of all of a father's wealth. This was an entitlement of the firstborn son. The firstborn would access his father's wealth only upon the death of his father. And as long as the father lived, the firstborn like every other child worked for the father. Potentially the firstborn owned everything. He had to grow up and mature before he could command the wealth.

Jacob was playing a dangerous game but Esau was so famished, he hardly knew or cared what was going on.

"Look here," said Esau, "Can't you see I'm dying of hunger? What use is my birthright to me?"

Jacob, who was a master in this negotiation, demanded that Esau gives his word to seal the deal.

Esau, without even thinking about the implications of his decision, hastily swore the oath. Pushing his brother aside, he devoured the soup with some bread to go with it.

He ate and drank his fill. Then he got up, satisfied and simply walked away. That is how little Esau cared about his birthright – his father's special blessing that would see him inherit his father's wealth.

In life, you are either a Jacob or an Esau. The '*Jacobs*' produce goods and services while the '*Esaus*' consume. These two characters define two classes of people in an economy, those who work to produce goods and services, and those who work to consume. Jacob used the implements in his environment skilfully to produce a finished product while Esau just hunted and never produced a consumable product.

Consumerism is defined as "the preoccupation of society with the acquisition of goods and service". We live in a world that in the literal analysis is driven by three words; eat, drink and cloth.

To respond to consumerism people in most cases have to go and look for a job so that they can earn some money. Like Esau, many people today act instinctively by just looking for employment. They don't take the time to critically think about what matters most to them.

The rat race of life is that the more money you earn the more you can buy and satisfy your daily needs, and the circle repeats day in day out. Remember in the story of Esau, all he cared for was satisfying his immediate need. He despised his birthright.

Consumerism is pushing millions of people to sell out their birthright. Do you know that you too have a birthright? How much do you care about your birthright? Do you know what your birthright is? Take time to think, what is the value of your birthright? Are you despising your birthday by getting a job?

## GET TO KNOW YOUR BIRTHRIGHT

You may have nothing today. You may even be stranded in unpleasant circumstances but you have the potential to become whatever you were created to become. Human potential is the ability of a person (individual) or humanity (a group of individuals) to put their theoretical abilities into practice.

The word "*potential*" comes from the Latin word "*potentia*" which means "*strength*". We can think of potential as a hidden opportunity, ability, strength, that can be displayed under enabling circumstances.

Your potential is your birthright. You are loaded with great abilities, talents, gifts, strengths by which you can become all you need to become in life. What you need to move from where you are to where you want to be is already in you.

The method God designed for man to actuate his potential is work. Through work, men manifest their potential. But like Esau and Jacob the type of work you do will either make you manifest your potential or inhibit it. The most important work you can do in life is the one which unveils to the world what God deposited in you. That's why you should begin to think seriously about your job.

Let's see how this story of Esau and Jacob further exemplifies two typical work and income systems.

## TWO DIAMETRICALLY OPPOSED WORK AND INCOME SYSTEMS

In most cases, people just work jobs without much thought of the underlying systems governing their field of work. The first and most popular system goes something like this; Go to school, get good grades, so you can get a "*good*" job, make lots of money, get a house mortgage, a car and get married, keep up with the Joneses, and be "*successful*".

People in this system never pause to ask if what they are doing is an expression of their full potential. What matters to them is getting salary and settling immediate needs. This group of workers is just engaged in jobs merely for the salary.

The point I am making here is that those people who work in this system are the "*Esaus*" that damn their birthright for a bowl of soup. That salary you are being given is the bowl of soup while you throw your potential in the trash can.

The second system is one in which people work to fulfill their potential. This system goes something like this; discover self, develop self through value addition, work in a job of your passion and earn money to work for you.

People in this system discover and make use of their potential to produce goods and services. The motivation for people in this system is not survival but fulfillment. It is sad to note that only about 3% of the world's population work in this system.

Allow me to share a story that illustrates these two systems in modern day situations. It is a fascinating story of one of America's accomplished entrepreneurs. Robert Kiyosaki tells his life story in his book **"Rich Dad Poor Dad"**, where these two systems are exemplified.

Robert went through 30 years learning journey about money. Robert's best friend Mike was an all-weather companion and the two of them went on this learning journey together. Robert had two dads; his biological father and his best friend's father. Mike's dad is the character Roberts refers to as *"rich dad"* and his biological father as *"poor dad"*.

His poor dad was a highly educated man, commanding a successful career with good earnings but yet poor.

On the other hand, rich dad never finished eighth grade and had no college degree. But through ardent hard work and a sound wealth mindset rich dad went on to become one of Hawaii's richest men.

Just like many parents, both of these men gave genuine advice to young Robert. But they advised different principles. Even on the same subject matter the two presented different advice.

They presented two diametrically opposed work and income systems.

For example, one would advise saying, *"Study hard so you can find a good company to work for"*. The other dad recommended, *"Study hard so you can find a good company to buy"*. Poor dad's advice, unfortunately, is what a lot of parents advice their children and it is killing their dreams and aspirations in life.

At age 9, Robert had to make a painful decision. That decision is the reason Robert is an icon of wealth today. Robert decided to listen and learn from his rich dad, consequently rejecting the advice of his poor dad, even though he was the one with all the college degrees.

Having made the decision Robert's journey about money begun, lasting for 30 years till he was 39 years old. Having been educated in the school of mastering money, Robert retired at 47 and went on to do what he enjoys most; investing.

Like most people in the Esau system, poor dad died living bills to be paid while rich dad died living millions of dollars to his family, charities, and church.

You see, it not just a matter of working. You need to study the system under which you are working.

Reader, are you aware of these two systems that govern work and means of income? Many people are so naive that they suspend critical thought about their jobs thus condemning themselves to employment servitude for life.

Are you among the poor and middle class who work in a system that never promotes or allows financial freedom? The poor work in a system that takes away from them the little they earn while the rich work in a system that multiplies what they earn, bringing them joy and according to them opportunities to engage in their passions and hobbies.

Can you confidently say you are in that clique of the rich who work in a system that produces wealth?

Despite all the degrees poor dad, like millions of people out there had no clue of the systems of work and income that exist. He was simply going through the motions. The rich employ money to sponsor their passions and hobbies while the poor work their whole life for money.

With the obsession of finding employment, you could be abandoning the things you are passionate about into enslavement. Don't end up in a job that will bore you to lunacy. Let me ask you the following questions:

1. What is your philosophy (belief and value system) regarding work and money?
2. Do you find security in just finding a job or you are free spirited and take risks?
3. Do you see your salary by itself as a means to your financial freedom?
4. Does your work accord you the freedom to think of new ways of doing things better?
5. Are you planning to retire early or you are only looking forward to retiring at the constitution stipulated age?
6. What dreams, passions and hobbies have you given up to do the job you are doing?
7. Do you wake up every morning thinking you could be doing something else than going to your current job?

8. Given another chance would you choose to do a different job?

I want you to take the time to honestly answer these questions before proceeding to read. Answering these questions will help you make meaningful benefit of the fore coming information. By the end of this reading, you should be able to comfortably answer the above questions and draw conclusions that will help you be free from employment servitude.

## WHY STAY IN A JOB YOU HATE

Myopia characterizing the workforce is lamentable, millions are led into willful slavery to a system that cripples their God-endowed ingenuity. In a 1968 issue of Harvard Business Review, Frederick Herzberg published a now-classic article titled "One More Time: How Do You Motivate Employees?" Herzberg wrote, "People are more satisfied with their jobs (and therefore must be motivated) when those jobs give them the opportunity to experience achievement. Thus to say a person must find something beyond mere work. That something is an achievement. People are motivated if they are able to evaluate their job in terms of achievement rather than salary.

> *"I've met and worked with many people who were less than enthusiastic about their jobs. Over the years I've heard all sorts of stories. Some remind me of my own. The ideal job that seemed so wonderful during the recruitment process turned out to be wrong on so many levels. There were times when a sense*

> *of unease disturbed an otherwise very happy*
> *working life and where the once perfect job*
> *changed drastically, usually due restruc-*
> *turing, and so my job satisfaction bottomed*
> *out. Each time I found myself asking that*
> *question, should I stay or should I go?"*
> *(Sharon Feltham)*

Sharon Feltham, like many people, reached rock bottom in her job, she began to ask herself; ***"should I stay or should I go"*** This soul-searching, personal inventory question initiates a painful process of confronting and working through all the fears and excuses that keep people stuck in jobs they were not born to do. If you stay longer than necessary in a job you hate, you will be a miserable worker. Like Sharon, serious self-examination by asking critical questions can help you to master the courage required to pursue your God-given dream. Have you come to that stage of asking yourself; ***"should I stay or should I go"***?

> *"I knew that any job I went to was*
> *going to make me miserable again"*
> *(Nasar El-Arabi)*

Doing work that does not align with your passion and life calling can psychologically, physically and emotionally be stressful. And stress can seriously affect your health and general well-being. No matter how much enthusiasm you have, working the wrong job will drain you eventually. You will soon change from being a happy dynamic professional to a half-hearted clock-watcher who rushes to the car park on the stroke of five. It's time to take control of your life. Why should you kill yourself doing jobs that you were never wired for? Why should you stay at a job the bores you into depression? It's time to reclaim your life back.

> *"I didn't see it then, but it turned out that getting fired from Apple was the best thing that could have ever happened to me. The heaviness of being successful was replaced by the lightness of being a beginner again, less sure about everything. It freed me to enter into one of the most creative periods of my life."*
> (Steve Jobs)

## "STOP WORKING FOR UNCLE SAM" IS A CHANCE TO BEING AGAIN

Most people consider job loss as the worst thing that could ever happen to them. But not so for Steve Jobs, after being ousted in a power struggle within Apple in 1984, just some 8 years after he'd founded the company, Steve Jobs did not slink off into dark corners to lick his wounds and wane and hurl expletives. Walking away from familiar shores to conquer new frontiers is always risky but often times if well calculated a rewarding undertaking. "You cannot discover new oceans unless you have the courage to loose sight of the shore" Steve found freedom away from Apple and entered into what he calls, "the most creative periods of my life". I believe if Steve Jobs didn't lose that job with Apple we wouldn't have all the wonderful inventions he brought about.

By gaining his freedom, Steve Jobs went on to revolutionize the motion picture industry. He bought Lucasfilm Computer Graphics for $10-million in 1986 and turning it into Pixar. Pixar became a recipient of more than two dozen Academy Awards and several billions of dollars in box office sales. That's the beauty of starting all over again. You get a chance of doing what you would otherwise have not accomplished. Jobs never stopped thinking differently. Leaving Apple meant setting himself free from the control of a system that limited his gift and imagination.

What if you woke up tomorrow and your boss told you that you were fired? Or suddenly you were laid off due to restructuring? Are you under constant fear that you may wake up someday to be told that your services are no longer required? Well, you don't have to be afraid anymore. This book is a manual to guide you step by step through the process of setting yourself free from employment servitude so you can do the job you love; the job you were created for.

Come to think of it, most of your day is spent at work or on activities related to your work. What a shame, wasting all those precious hours doing what you dislike.

National certified career counselors and life coach Kelvin and Kay Brennfleck say that about 60% or more of people's lives are spent working. That leaves you with little or no time at all to engage in your life calling. That time you could be spending doing the will and purpose of God or being with loved ones is spent wasting away your life for survival.

As Elbert Hubbard said, "The greatest mistake you can make in life is continually fearing that you'll make one".

Your desire to be free to do what you love doing is not

a mistake. But you will certainly be making a mistake if you continue in the wrong job fearing that you may be making one by quitting. You have a choice, to break free from this system of bondage.

*"Stop working for Uncle Sam"*, relating to the words of Steve Jobs is, therefore "lightness of being a beginner again". You too can begin again. You can make that escape. You have a chance to regain your life back, therefore stop postponing your escape, be bold and take that step and stop working for Uncle Sam.

*"Though no man can go back and make a brand new start, anyone can start from now and make a brand new ending"*. You can start afresh from where you are today. This book is my heartfelt concern for you who may be trapped in a system that limits your true potential and purpose. This is my message of freedom to people who are employment slaves in a system that doesn't care about them living a purposeful and fulfilling life.

As I travel the world, most especially to America, and London; I have seen often with a sad heart the millions of people trapped in the rat race. These are people who could have contributed immensely to making this world a better place by focusing on work that expresses their true self. But they have bargained for cheap existence. Merely working for a salary, shame!

The information contained in this book will clearly teach you all you need to know about this modern system of slavery and how you could be set free. You will be further enlightened on God's plan for your life regarding work.

Millions untold have been and are still being educated to be enlisted into this wicked system. *"Stop working for*

*Uncle Sam"* presents a paradigm shift in your education. Uncle Sam is a wicked system because it depreciates an individual's resources leaving them to utter shame in old age retirement.

If you keep working under the yoke of this worldly system you can't and will never serve God freely and fully.

Dr. Martin Luther King Jr. said in his historic speech at Lincoln Memorial, *"The whirlwinds of revolt will continue to shake the foundations of our nation until the bright day of justice emerges".* In like manner, in your quest to stop working for Uncle Sam and gaining your freedom to serve God in your given field of calling, may the whirlwinds of revolt never cease.

# PART I

## UNDERSTANDING UNCLE SAM SYSTEM

## CHAPTER ONE

# WHO IS UNCLE SAM?

Born to answer a particular cry of humanity, does your job enable you to achieve that? Are you fulfilling your God-given dream? It's a crime against humanity for you to die without adding your solution to this world. In this chapter, I will put forth truths that expose this wicked system.

**"Uncle Sam"** is a popular term that depicts government's dominion over its citizens through employment, tax charges, and many other statutory obligations. By the term Uncle Sam, I am referring to any system that captivates you, or where you work in order to merely make money and survive. Thus Uncle Sam is any system that is only giving you a means of survival and not fulfillment.

Allow me to narrate briefly the history behind the term "Uncle Sam", For the sake of readers who may have no idea of the personification of the United States of American government as Uncle Sam. In 1813, the United States got its nickname, Uncle Sam, from a meat-packer from Troy, New York. Samuel Wilson was his name. He supplied barrels of beef to the United States Army during the War of 1812.

Wilson was a well-liked and trustworthy man in Troy, and local residents called him "Uncle Sam. "Wilson (1766-1854) stamped the barrels with "U.S." for the United States, but the soldiers began referring to the grub as "Uncle Sam's." The local newspaper picked up on the story and Uncle Sam eventually gained widespread acceptance as the nickname for the U.S. federal government".

"In September 1961, the USA congress recognized Samuel Wilson as "the progenitor of America's national symbol of Uncle Sam". Wilson died at age 88 in 1854, and was buried next to his wife Betsey Mann in the Oakwood Cemetery in Troy, New York, the town that calls itself "The home of Uncle Sam". Uncle Sam started appearing in images and literature soon after the war of 1812. Uncle Sam was popularized in the late 19th century in political cartoons by one of America's well-known cartoonist, Thomas Nast. However, the 1977 recruiting poster of Uncle Sam asking "YOU" to join the army is perhaps the most enduring rendition of the character.

## YOUR TIME IS YOUR LIFE

When 20 years of your life is elapsed, will you look back in regret recounting what you could have done but didn't do? You must realize that every second, counts, so make the most of it.

Roy Coops worked at a large Fitness Company that paid him a good salary, provided him with a car, laptop, and mobile phone. Roy had to work 7 days a week and every day he spent 10 hours at the job. 10 hour a day, 7 days a week, it was hard work for sure.

The company was a sales driven company, thus, as long as Roy created good 'numbers' his job was secure. Roy realized that the pursuit of the good 'numbers' meant that people who already joined the club didn't get the attention they needed and consequently left.

Against the company philosophy, Roy preferred to embrace the existing members instead of the stress of gaining enough new members. As time went by, Roy, fell out of favor with his employers. He wasn't useful to the company anymore. As a result, he got kicked out of the company in a bad way.

It was after being kicked out of his job that Roy resolved that he would never give a huge part of his time a company that doesn't care about anyone but only themselves. You, my reader, don't have to wait to be fired to realize that Uncle Sam is stealing your time.

That decision to revolt against the slavery of working a job he didn't like bought him back precious hours to engage in his passion. During his employment, he only had to do that which pleased his employers and not what was deep down his soul.

After being fired, Roy started his own company but he didn't earn much money, so he had to find himself another job. It was a part-time job, working 3 days a week. The job gave Roy the opportunity to earn enough money to pay bills and still have 4 days to work on his own business.

Somehow, Roy couldn't just find the perfect combination between the part-time job and his business.

He needed more time to focus on his business.

The pressure for survival was getting to Roy. Roy was burdened with questions like, how he was going to make enough money, what if he spent all his saving in the process of building his business, how would he provide home necessities etc. What would he do if his business didn't work out? The pressure weighed even heavier than before. But at the same time, the desire to take control of his own life grew bigger, and bigger and out-weighed his fears.

One thing was sure for Roy, there was no turning back.

Roy Coops says if he still worked as an employee in some company, he would live his life structured by society and for his boss' wallet, and not being able to do the things he loves. *"I think I still wouldn't know what I love to do and would not have the time to discover and explore them"*.

The lesson from this story is that *"time is the currency of life thus time wasters are life wasters"*.

If you are working by getting instructions about what to and not what to do, you are a slave to Uncle Sam. If you are constantly being wrongfully reprimanded or castigated for one thing or another then it's time to rethink your job. That's the agony of working in a slave system like Uncle Sam system.

The truth is that very few people are in control of their lives. Governments and company owners, by and large, are controlling many people today.

Most people never commit wholeheartedly to resigning from the jobs that restrict their God-given freedoms, talents, and gifts. But you must find that courage and take that bold step. It is time to find your freedom. Go after your God-given dreams.

Here are some critical lessons from Roy's story about Uncle Sam system:

- Employers never care about you but about making profits.
- Following your passion means being unpopular with your employers.
- You must take a firm decision to redeem and protect your time.
- You need to be free from the system that keeps

you in bondage, never allowing you to do what you love.

- To remain free, you require 100% focus and full-time engagement to turn your business, hobby or passion into a growing venture.

The story of Roy Coop illustrates what most people are going through in the quest to make a living. People by the millions are going to get employed in establishments owned by the government and company shareholders. The citizenry looks forward to being employed in the system so that they would earn a salary for meeting their daily needs.

Uncle Sam system defines an economic system in which trade and industry are controlled by the state and private owners for profit. Whether it is the state, private or self-owned, any system that limits people's self-expression in work and takes away their liberties and freedoms is Uncle Sam. If your job is solely for salary it is clear that you are working for Uncle Sam.

Do you realize that your job could be robbing you of the time required to discover your life's calling and purpose? Don't allow the fear of failure to meet your daily needs paralyze your efforts in following after your dreams.

## ANATOMY OF UNCLE SAM BONDAGE

Unfortunately, people feel trapped by forces beyond their control, trapped in meaningless jobs, for the sake of money, status or recognition. Employers promise a salary that is just enough to keep you going back, thus making you dependent on the system for life. Is your livelihood completely dependent on the wage you earn?

Without any savings or investment, people are constantly living in fear of a life without a salary. If all you know and have as a means of Income is a salary, you are under Uncle Sam.

Uncle Sam system is structured in such a way that your prospects of leaving the system are spelled out in very harsh punitive realities like failure to pay bills, hunger, the lack of access to medical care and a gloomy dark old age with no pension etc.

What is even more painful is that Uncle Sam will pay you a salary and then you will have to contribute statutory emoluments back to Uncle Sam through Taxes. Governments, empowered by enacted laws require a compulsory contribution to state revenue from personal income and business profits or added to the cost of some goods, services, and transaction. Thus, on every purchase the government gets to tax and on every income or profit gained, taxes apply. Whether you are earning or spending, your allegiance is largely to Uncle Sam through taxes. Let's turn our attention to understanding Uncle Sam system in its inference in this discourse.

The ideology underlined in this book is that Uncle Sam is coined to symbolize the government's dominant system over its people. I am referring to the oppressive dominion of governments on its citizens. When you are working for Uncle Sam system you are at the mercy of the government for survival. You get employed for a salary and in exchange, you sell out your liberties, passions, and dreams. Oppression is real, as those who work for Uncle Sam are always under constant pressure to work in order to make ends meet.

Furthermore, Uncle Sam system typifies any kind of dependence on any system, organization or person that makes you look up to it/them for employment or survival.

The trauma people went through during the recent recession is just one of the many indicators of dependence on Uncle Sam.

According to Bureau of Labor Statistics accessing the impact of the recent recession where an estimated 8.8 Million jobs were lost says that:

- Most middle-aged people were disproportionately affected in terms of lost property value, household finances, and lost retirement savings.
- 27% of those aged 50 to 64 experienced reductions in salaries, a percentage higher than any other age group.
- Of those middle-aged workers who committed suicide from 2005 to 2010, 81 percent had prior mental health or substance abuse problems.

These bizarre statistics exemplify the bondage of millions who depended on Uncle Sam system. Thus many individuals working in Uncle Sam system are under so much pressure that results in depression, substance abuse and in some cases ending up in suicide. When you get employed by Uncle Sam, you totally dependent on the system, you become a slave to the system.

When you are at the mercy of other people who are at the top of the social, financial or corporate ladder you are living in the bondage employment servitude. Uncle Sam is the modern form of slavery. It is utter human exploitation.

Uncle Sam is a system of bondage structured around a society of meeting needs and wants thereby restricting and controlling people's liberties. You are no longer living the life God purposed for you. Rather your life is now programmed by society, religion, and media, simply living for other people and not for your creator.

The bondage of Uncle Sam is established through various forms which include employment, credit cards, mortgages, various forms of insurance, taxes etc. These vices have brought a heavy burden of bondage on people. People cannot live free but are forever tied to the system for survival. Burdened by mortgages, loans, credit card or student debt or nearing retirement some employees feel that they can't afford to leave their jobs. In many cases longer serving and accomplished employees in Uncle Sam system who earn higher than average salaries often realize it's unlikely they'll find another job with a matching salary out there. Reluctantly many of them would rather not compromise their standard of living and would rather remain under Uncle Sam system.

Let us consider a popular example of Uncle Sam's bondage, the car ownership deals of most Americans. Let's examine three questions provided by the Bureau of Security and Investigative Services (BISI) regarding car repossession.

1. What does a contract have to do with car repossession?
2. What happens if you miss a payment on your loan?
3. What if you don't claim the repossessed vehicle?

The answers given by the Bureau should be appreciated as mind opening, helping us to vividly highlight the slavery of working for Uncle Sam.

Responding to the first question the bureau writes; "When you sign a contract for a secured loan to buy a car, boat, motorcycle, RV or other merchandise, you agree to make payments and meet the terms of the contract. The terms may include the seller's (or legal owner's) right to repossess that collateral if you don't make the payments". The system encourages people to get these loans whose burden of repayment can last as long as 20 or more years in installments.

Secondly, should one default payment terms, the bureau advice that "your contract may allow a grace period during which you can still make a payment without having your collateral repossessed. However, the legal owner can repossess your collateral at any time after the first day you miss a payment, depending on the terms and conditions of your contract. Even if you make payments on time, your vehicle could still be repossessed if you do not meet other terms of the contract, such as insurance". It is those hidden clauses which are not obvious to the people that are the heartbreaking realities that lead to repossession of collateral. Most often, when a person is out of employment even just for a month most of them will miss a payment. Thus in most cases, people are never thinking about living their jobs no matter what.

And lastly in the event that you don't claim the repossessed item, "you may still be liable for the balance due on your loan contract, plus storage fees and other costs associated with the repossession. This loan system is not meant to make people live comfortably rather keep them in the continued bondage of working for Uncle Sam. People stay in jobs so that they can continue to meet these mortgage, loan and credit obligations thus reducing people to economic slaves.

Willingly people take up these contracts which they work to repay all their lives. These vices are the modern chains of bondage and slavery; far worse than the enslavement of the African people in past centuries. It is worse because people are willingly selling out themselves to the system for small, meager benefits of promised salary to enable them meet their needs and pay off their loan, credit card and mortgage obligations.

In the past, African slaves had no option. To survive they had to work in various plantations and establishments just to eat and cloth. Today people on their own accord take themselves into slavery to Uncle Sam just for a salary.

## ARE YOU IMPRISONED IN YOUR JOB?

Furthermore, Uncle Sam is any job or profession that ties you down and deprives you of your will and freedom. If you have to keep committing to and rendering your allegiance to a particular organization or system for continued salary and survival, you are under the bondage. You must know that every time you come under compulsion to make a living and find means of survival, you bring yourself under the bondage of Uncle Sam. People are living in houses, driving cars, wearing clothes and getting an education on Loan. This is living an artificial life.

The pressure to work for a salary for a person trapped

in this system is almost unavoidable as the person sees no other way out. It is obvious that when you are under Uncle Sam system you don't make decisions as to when you take a vacation or stop work if you so desire.

When others are doing all they can to stay in the system it is almost unthinkable to take a vacation. Well, NBA icon Jrue Holiday does just that. Just before the start of the 2016 – 17 season, Jrue has had to take leave. He had to go on leave to attend to the person who matters to him the most; his wife. Jrue Holiday took an indefinite leave from the NBA New Orleans Pelicans to care for his wife who is carrying his child. Holiday's wife, apart from being pregnant had been diagnosed with brain tumor. Jrue's coach remarked, *"The most important thing for Jrue to do right now is to be with his wife and family"*.

A person can only take such a step if he is free from the system. Very few people can take a vacation at will because many have sold themselves to the system. They are totally dependent on the system for survival.

Jrue could take leave because he needed to and not because the system made him to. How many people have that freedom to take a vacation when they want to? Do you my reader have that freedom? People under Uncle Sam's bondage are never allowed free time to indulge in activities that promote their own lives outside their work.

In most cases, workers desiring to take vacation are usually threatened with being blacklisted for promotion. Other employers will even tell their workers that in times of downsizing, it is usually those who take their right to vacation that gets laid off.

So many people get excited about signing a new job

contract; little do they know that they are selling themselves out to Uncle Sam system. There is a gospel song with lyrics; *"I pledge allegiance to the Lamb"*. The sad reality is that individuals in their millions have pledged allegiance to Uncle Sam system for survival at the expense of living their God-ordained purpose.

Occasionally those who try to live free from Uncle Sam by way of self-employment in business ventures end up creating a system that enslaves them. This is due to the lack of knowledge of what it takes to be free from this unforgiving worldly system. Starting business ventures as a means of survival is also living under Uncle Sam.

Your goal in starting a business must be to gain freedom from enslavement so that you can serve the Lord Jesus Christ where and when he sends you.

Keep in mind, Uncle Sam is a government, corporation, system or person; that includes self, which is created to secure and appease people's need for survival by giving them a salary.

Uncle Sam system is no longer a western or European phenomenon but it is the character of modern society world over. Even in Africa, Uncle Sam is a vivid reality that is seeing the rich few, controlling and managing the wealth of nations while multitudes wallow in poverty.

Social security, Credit card, mortgage and many other systems appear to be the way of living the good life most especially in the West but all that is Uncle Sam at work; exploiting and strengthening its bondage on God's people.

The reality is that most Americans today live for other people, working so hard paying off debts and performing jobs dictated by others.

The term slave or servant sounds harsh but that is what you are when you are employed in a job variant to your purpose. Uncle Sam is a sophisticated mechanism of modern enslavement.

Let me illustrate this slavery by giving another insert from Tyler Durden. Tyler writes *"Today when you add up a; mortgage debt, all credit card debt and all student loan debt the average American household is carrying a grand total of 203,163 dollars. Overall, American households are more than 11 trillion in debt at this point. And even though most Americans don't realize this, over the course of our lifetimes the amount of money that we will repay on our debts is far greater than the amount we originally borrowed. In fact, when it comes to credit card debt you can easily end up repaying several times the amount of money that you originally borrowed. So we work our fingers to the bone to pay off these debts, and the vast majority of us are not even working for ourselves. Instead, our work makes the businesses that other people own more profitable. So if we spend the best years of our lives building businesses for others, serving debts that we owe to others and making them wealthier, what does that make us?"* that makes us slaves and servants. Who are you enriching through your job?

Looking at how your life is being spent, simply creating wealth for others. By what I have already said, we can deduce clearly the following.

You are under Uncle Sam's bondage when you are:

- Spending your life working for others by building other people's businesses.
- Working to pay off a debt you owe.

- Motivated to work only for monetary compensation.
- Performing tasks that others tell you that you "must" do as opposed to what makes you happy.
- Working to make other people wealthier.
- Abandoning and sacrificing your dreams for salary.
- Living paycheck to paycheck.
- Unable to sustain your life and family without a salary.
- Spending money you don't have using credit cards, loan, and mortgage.
- Constantly having no time to pursue what is really important to you.
- Spending so much energy, time and focus on a job that you hardly have anything left over for your life's calling.
- Through these summary points, I challenge you to analyze your life to see if you are truly free from modern servitude.

## EDUCATION – ANOTHER MECHA-NISM OF UNCLE SAM BONDAGE

For most people, the ideal life perceives a college education as one of the most promising avenues to attaining a life of affluence. With soaring student loan debt and shortages of jobs, a crisis is emanating for sure. Thus those who see education as a stable vehicle to living the good life i.e. American dream should think again.

Through the education system, Uncle Sam teaches

people to work for the system and never to think of freedom that comes from working in the place of your calling and passion.

In the United Kingdom, for instance, various government and non-government institutions have been established for the purpose of providing loans to students. E.g. Student Loans Company (SLC) which is a non-profit-making organization, providing loans and grants to students in universities and colleges on behalf of the UK Government and the administrations of Scotland, Wales and Northern Ireland. Students are given a chance to earn an education through these loans. Without realizing it these loans become a means through which people are enslaved. When a student finishes their education the burden of servicing the loans still is heavy.

The systems are established in such a way that when the time comes for one to repay their student loan, the Student Loans Company will work with the Revenue and Customs authorities to collect the loan repayments. This repayment period lasts very long, thus denying the individual the opportunity to save money and later invest it towards financial freedom. Thus a student earning an education by way of a loan is damned to employment servitude. But through a superior knowledge such a person can find freedom. This book gives you that superior knowledge.

## TAKE ANOTHER LOOK AT YOUR PAY SLIP

Otherwise called a pay statement, a pay slip is that summary of your income and statutory deductions per remuneration period. The cardinal question worth pondering is; *"where does your income or salary go to"?* After you gain your salary it's almost as if it is on an escapes mission from your hands. Let me ask you, who makes the decisions on your income? You may think you are in charge but the truth is that; it is Uncle Sam who is making your financial decisions. Just look at the 'deductions' section of that pay advice and you will agree.

If at the end of the day you can't account for much of your income, it is a clear sign that you are working for and living under Uncle Sam system. Your salary is spent by Uncle Sam even before it reaches your hands.

Tax deductions, pension fund deductions, medical, funeral and other forms of insurance all get their share of your hard earned money before giving the remainder to you for further distribution to other demands. House rent and other bills also claim the remaining amount and then you have to go through the monthly motions all over again; what a sad way of living your life when you can do more to honor and glorify God with it. Have you noticed that your money disappears faster than when you receive your next salary? You have to realize that it's no longer the system working for you but you working hard for the system. Most benefits of your hard work in Uncle Sam system go to the system living you with only peanuts. Let's look at a few facts that apply to salaried workers:

- Up to about 40% to 50% of your salary goes to taxes. Typically these taxes fall under Income taxes, social security, and Medicare

- Popular to Americans, about 10% to 20% goes to paying off your mortgage,
- Another 10% or also goes to pay off student loans.
- About another 5% to 8% goes to taxes on everything you consume.

This is even before you pay for rent and other bills.

If we add other insurance deductions and social security contributions a person remains with less than 20% from his salary. At the minimum, a salaried worker loses about 60% of his income to the system. The truth is that the total value you create for your employer doesn't all come to you. Some of it is what goes to pay your bosses, shareholders, and paying for office maintenance etc.

Whilst you work hard to pay other people, the rich people in America, for example, pay less than 15% on average on their gains in their net worth. The point is this; people working for Uncle Sam are simply slaves working to enrich others.

Uncle Sam deprives people of their God given liberties and freedoms. The will to make decisions as to what the individual wants and desires in life is surrendered to the system. This is the injustice and cruelty of Uncle Sam system; it does not care about what really makes you happy or fulfilled. Your only reward in Uncle Sam system is a salary that hardly gets you through the month.

Wake up and realize who you are working for. It's not God, yourself, your family or loved ones but Uncle Sam whom you are serving. Every minute you spend working for Uncle Sam is a minute you are dying to your dreams. Norman Cousines says, "Death is not the greatest loss in life. The greatest loss is what dies inside us while we live". The question to you is this, what is dying on the inside of you because you keep going to work for your employer?

*"Our lives begin to end the day we become silent about things that matter"*
*(Martin Luther King, Jr.)*

# CHAPTER 1
# GOLDEN POINTS

1. Uncle Sam symbolizes the government's dominion system over its people. It is the oppressive dominion of the government of the citizens.

2. Uncle Sam system typifies any kind of dependence on any system, organization or individual that makes people look up to them for employment and survival.

3. Whether state, private or self-owned, any system that limits and takes away people's freedoms and liberties is Uncle Sam.

4. Every time you come under compulsion to make a living and find means of survival, you bring yourself under the bondage of Uncle Sam.

5. Your only reward for working for Uncle Sam is salary; that hardly gets you through the month.

CHAPTER TWO

# LIFE CYCLE IN UNCLE SAM SYSTEM

It is important to enshrine in our minds the knowledge of Uncle Sam system in our quest for independence from this modern slavery. As Thomas Jefferson said, "Nothing can stop the man with the right mental attitude from achieving his goals; *"Nothing on earth can help the man with the wrong mental attitude"*. If you are ignorant about the system that is enslaving you, then you are helpless; far from emancipation. This knowledge about Uncle Sam is one of the fundamentals for one to move from poverty into a life of freedom. That is, freedom to follow your dreams and life calling.

*"Lifecycle"* is just a phrase am using in this book to express the various stages and players in this system. The life cycle typifies the stages of life and the changes a person undergoes while working for Uncle Sam. There is a metamorphic life journey as a person works through the system. It starts off in a high gear but diminishes gradually. There is always an emotional and attitude change working in Uncle Sam system. Let's turn our attention for now to identifying these players in Uncle Sam system.

### 1. UNCLE SAM – THE BIG BROTHER

The first player in the system is 'Uncle Sam'. By now you have a clear understanding of who Uncle Sam is. Remember, it is any kind of dependence on any system, organization or person that makes you look up to it or them for employment or survival. We have so far established that Uncle Sam could represent a person (including self), government, organization or a system. The fact that most people don't even know that there is Uncle Sam system running their lives is a painful reality.

Uncle Sam is the big brother who is watching your every move, monitoring and influencing your decisions and actions to keep you under his bondage.

It is obvious that Governments strive by all means to retain their control over citizens.

In the USA for example:

Under the welfare reform law passed in 1996, employers are compelled to report identifying information about all new employees for inclusion in a massive federal database.

The health insurance portability and accountability Act of 1996 mandated a new federal medical record database, and policy insists on the right to view that information with a warrant.

Governments always finds a justifiable reason for such controls. This is to qualify the point, that governments, employers, and other institutions typify a system of bondage restricting people's freedoms at various levels.

Even though people claim to be free to follow their dreams, there always seems to be an invisible hand that controls their lives.

## 2. THE ENSLAVED MASSES

The second player is *"YOU"* and the millions of people that have been enslaved in the system. Some of the people are enslaved in Uncle Sam system with eyes wide open and others blinded by Uncle Sam's bait and advertising schemes. You are created in the image of God for a purpose. God made each man uniquely to be a solution to a problem in their generation. Instead of pursuing that purpose people end up being trapped in Uncle Sam system because of the desire to make a living. Your purpose is bigger than just working a regular job. Your life purpose is not to merely make a living. You have a divine purpose and everything you do should be in the pursuit of that purpose. Do you know that you have a purpose in life beyond earning a salary? Are you either living that purpose or you merely existing?

The International Labor Organization, in the World Employment Social Outlook – 2015 Trends publication said that bulks of new jobs are being created in private sector services. The private sector services will employ more than a third of the global workforce over the next five years. The publication revealed the following:

- Industrial employment is expected to stabilize globally at slightly below 22% of total employment.

- Public services in health care, education and administration will see a smaller increase around 12% of total employment.

- High-skilled non-routine jobs have been increasing steadily, making up more than 18% of total employment.

- The advanced economies still account for the largest share of manufacturing jobs across the global. Current trends will bring their employment share to below 12% by the end of 2019.

As the indicators show us, there will certainly be a

job for you out there but the cardinal question is this, will it be the right job for you? With a steady increase in occupational and sectoral employment patterns, many people are sure to damn their freedoms for the opportunity of earning a salary.

These statistics observed by ILO show globally how the system of Uncle Sam is growing thus broadening its grip on the masses. These prospect job opportunities spell out new enslavement avenues if people don't learn how to work in the system without being under its bondage.

### 3. THE PROMISE FOR WORKING FOR UNCLE SAM

The third component of the life cycle is the promise; the bait. Why is it that as harsh as Uncle Sam system is, people never seem to revolt against it to find their freedom? The truth is that there is a promise that makes people forget all about the need for freedom. People hope to attain freedom through hard work in Uncle Sam system. The promise of freedom in Uncle Sam is simply a salary. The mindset of people in Uncle Sam system is that if they work harder and harder they will be able to earn enough to live free. But the opposite is true, no matter how much you earn in Uncle Sam system your salary will not bring you into freedom if you remain in the system. This component is discussed further in a later chapter called Uncle Sam's bait. People are selling themselves out to Uncle Sam for mainly two things. Firstly, the opportunity to earn a salary for meeting daily needs and secondly, the illusory security of having a stable job and retirement funds. There is much more to your life than salary and pension. The truth is that God will demand an account from you on the gifts and talents he puts in you so wake up and get busy working on your life's calling.

## 4. THE PARALYZING FEAR OF UNMET NEEDS

*"A life lived in fear is a life half lived".*
*(Baz Luhrmann)*

Another component of Uncle Sam system is **"FEAR"**. Uncle Sam system works on instilling fear in people. Common fears are; that you won't afford to send your children to school, fear that you won't manage to pay your house rent if you don't keep earning a salary etc. Even though people don't want to admit it; they are living in slavery. The spirit of bondage under Uncle Sam system brings people under a dark cloud of fear. The harsh reality for most people is that if they were out of employment just for three months they would end up hungry, homeless and struggling. Fearing that dilemma, most people would rather continue in employment servitude. It is fear that will incapacitate your efforts of trying to work outside the system. The fear appears as a genuine, justifiable concern because what a person fears seems rational and morally right. Let me tell you a story to illustrate this point.

Jason Spencer's business had just collapsed. And just about when his family savings buffer was completely gone, he had been introduced to an opportunity that looked like it would change everything. Jason worked on that project for 6 months then he received a phone call that the company was out of money, and that they wouldn't be able to pay him to keep going on the project.

He says, *"It was like a bomb went off. I was laid off, and out of work… just like that"*.

Jason narrates, *"I was not prepared. I didn't have enough time to prepare"*. His savings were exhausted from his failed business the previous year. For 6 months Jason worked on a bare bones salary just to pay the bills and get the company to launch. What was he going to do? "My wife. My kids. They depend on me, and I've got nothing left". Like Jason, these are the concerns most people have.

Imagine the pressure thousands of people like Jason have to go through. It is that fear of failure to meet needs of the family that makes people end up just working for Uncle Sam. The thought of his wife and kids became the driving thought and such sentimentality is what leads many to be enslaved by Uncle Sam. His motivation for work was wrong just like the millions out there wasting away their precious lives working for Uncle Sam.

## 5. THE DECEPTION THAT LEADS TO CHASING SHADOWS

The fifth component of Uncle Sam is the **"ILLU-SION"**. Similar to the promise the illusion is the hope of independence by working for Uncle Sam system. The illusion is usually a long-term focus. The illusion is that, if you continue to work hard and study harder and get more qualifications you will eventually be able to live the good life; free to follow your dreams.

In America, the illusion is coined in the statement, *"The American Dream"* which says that a person can come from nothing to become great. Thus America has the hardest working people on the planet. These people are hoping to achieve the American dream not realizing that in reality only a fraction of the population ever experiences that American dream.

In 2014, 'Business Insider' featured an article by Matthew Schiffman Head of Global Marketing at Legg Mason on the American dream. In the article, some 500 affluent Americans were asked to define the American dream. The following were summarized as what makes up the American dream:

- Feeling financially secure
- Having the freedom to live the way you want to
- Being able to retire at 65 and live comfortably in old age
- Owning your own home
- Knowing that working hard pays off

As you have seen the 5 goals highlighted in the survey have become the motivation behind people's jobs. To attain this, people are encouraged to get jobs, work hard and then get the money they have not earned. In getting Loans and mortgages they continue to work all their lives in order to pay back. The historical narrative reveals that an obvious indicator of a civilization in decline is that its people lose the capacity to delay gratification for the sake of the future. When asked whether the American dream is attainable:

- The majority (55%) of affluent investors said the American Dream is no longer within reach, with women (62%) more likely to say so than men (48%).
- 62% of Baby Boomers – ages 55 to 64 - believe the Dream is unattainable.
- 64% of investors with household incomes of

$250,000 or more also said the American Dream is no longer within reach.

- Only 23% "strongly agreed" that they were living the American Dream; just 36% of the 250 millionaires surveyed also "strongly agreed."

The aspiration for living the American dream brings many people into the debt trap. People accumulate some much consumer debt that the prospects of stopping conventional work are undreamed-of. They have to work all their life to pay off the debt.

Just take an evening to watch TV and you will see how Uncle Sam, through vicious strategic advertising, paints the picture of a good life before its victims so as to influence their decisions on the remaining income after statutory financial obligations are deducted.

There is an over-indulgence in consumerism (the preoccupation of society with the acquisition of goods) which has been nurtured and fed by Uncle Sam system. People's attitudes and actions regarding money are largely influenced too strongly by the desire to earn money or acquire more goods.

House, money, car and the like, flash continually, sending the masses into a spending frenzy. As a result, an unhealthy greed and appetite are created in people that lead them into a spending spree once money gets into their hands. A big house, a fancy sporting car, the latest phone or computer etc. and by the time you buy that new item another product on the market; better, fancy, faster, bigger and definitely requiring a little more cash is introduced. So this greed sets people on a journey of acquiring luxuries: a mere mirage that can never be satisfied and a future that is unobtainable.

# WHAT UNCLE SAM SYSTEM TEACHES?

The world system is structured in such a way that the only thing it teaches you about money is how to spend it. Uncle Sam financial education never teaches you how to rule or become a master over money but only how to spend. The more you spend the more you are subjugated to the power of money. Employers pay you a salary that you go on to spend in their shops and corporations. They encourage people to spend knowing the money is returning back to them.

Do you know that Advertising is a very costly business variable? But its benefits are so overwhelming that owners of businesses cannot do without it. Beware of Uncle Sam's enticements. You must be aware of Uncle Sam vices and avoid them always. Don't be under pressure to catch up popular trends. You will feel this pressure constantly but you must master the trickery of Uncle Sam. You've got to outsmart this wicked system and live free.

# EXPERIENCING THE AWAKENING

*"Experience is not what happens to a man. It is what a man does with what happens to him"*
*(Aldous Huxley)*

As people progress on in this rat race, a light shines on them and they awake to the reality of Uncle Sam system's egregiousness. But usually, the awakening takes place at a time when it is too late to divorce from the system. Many people end up frustrated and live in the perpetual complaint of how life has been so unfair. The awakening takes place in the later years of an individual's work in Uncle Sam system that it only gives birth to complaining and regret. As Mark Twain says, *"Twenty years from now you will be more disappointed by the things you didn't do than the ones you did do..."*

If you stay in the system longer than necessary, you will end up disappointed with what you had been doing with your life. The system strives to keep its victims blinded, preventing them from ever learning the laws of money which are a fundamental key to gaining freedom. This awaking to Uncle Sam slavery in most cases does no good because it never educates the younger generation nor can it master strength to help the individual break free from Uncle Sam system. What is left is a miserable unfulfilled life till death.

## STRENGTHENING THE BONDAGE THROUGH EDUCATION

Lastly, Uncle Sam cycle is planned in such a way that no matter the late awaking of victims, the light is never seen by upcoming generations. Uncle Sam system operates the world's education system. Thus the system works at injecting free blood into the system. From generation to generation Uncle Sam is educating people to perpetually work in the system. The people will never be taught the laws of money; they will be earning a salary with no clue of how money works. Through the education system, Uncle Sam succeeds in blinding people from the truth about principles and laws of money thereby sustaining the system. So, as long as the world system is educating you and your children in money matters, you will remain in slavery and your children will grow up to work as slaves under the bondage of Uncle Sam.

## YOUR LIFE'S METAMORPHOSIS

The purity of a childhood dream is simply admirable. All of us once had a dream. Probably your own dream was to become the president of your country. Perhaps your childhood dream was to one day set your foot on the moon. There is nothing as pure and innocent as a childhood dream.

But as we go along the path of life, we lose those precious dreams and just hope to live like everybody we see around us.

Typically life starts off with that childhood dream. Between the ages of 5 to 7 you dreamed of becoming something that you probably have buried since. Children are much close to their creator; innocent of the pollution of this worldly system. As a child, you didn't worry about where the money to achieve your dreams would come from. With only parents for your connections, you still dream big. Are you living your childhood dreamt or maybe you consider it as outrageous? Let me illustrate this point by sharing the story of Merlin with you.

As a young girl, Merlin dreamt of one day becoming a medical doctor. She would pretend to be taking the temperature of her patient; her elder brother who always felt bothered by her "doctor" games. Merlin didn't for a moment think of college or tuition fees; the only thing on her mind was her medical practice.

By the end of high school, the 18-year-old "doctor" Merlin had somehow forgotten all about her childhood dream. She was preoccupied with catching up with popular fashion trends, getting the attention of the popular boys at school; she simply wanted to fit in.

She was so preoccupied with being noticed.

Going along that path, it dawned on her that those with good jobs seemed to get that kind of life cheaply. They would afford the make-up, designer clothes, and latest shoes. And with that came all the attention. Merlin too was going to have that life.

What Merlin was pursuing now was getting a college degree and finding a good job thereafter. The elusive desires of youth had diminished that pure childhood dream of becoming a doctor. It didn't matter anymore, doctor, plumber or teacher, as long as she got a good salary to live the life she wanted.

At age 24, "doctor" Merlin worked at a bank as a teller. Her salary was attractive but it couldn't meet all her expenses. She was dreaming of purchasing her own apartment, get married and settle down. As a banker, she understood that her job made her credit worthy.

So Merlin got a mortgage for an apartment and she felt happy having her own home. She went on to get a car loan to ease her mobility. Merlin didn't seem to care that all this credit would take about 25 years to pay off. All that mattered was that she was in employment and getting a salary.

Happily married with two kids, "doctor" Merlin at age 30 was now dreaming of climbing the corporate ladder. She is now working so hard trying to win favors from top management. She dreams of one day being the section manager. There are two things that seem to cloud her mind right now. These are promotion and vacation.

She would say to her husband, *"honey? I deserve a break from all this hard work".* The dream of becoming a doctor, unfortunately, had been reduced to promotion and vacation, what a shame!

By age 45 the once vibrant Merlin is slowly seeing her life rapidly aging away. Joan Baez once said, *"You don't get to choose how you're going to die, only how you're going to live".* Merlin like many other people today had chosen to abandon her childhood dream. My dear reader, how are you choosing to live your life? Are you truly living your dream?

Merlin was now hoping her daughter would become a medical doctor. Merlin would always force her child to play the game she played as a child. Merlin is dreaming of one day seeing her children living the dream she lost along the journey of life.

**"So remember your Creator during your youth! Otherwise, troublesome days will come and years will creep up on you when you'll say, "I find no pleasure in them,"**

*Ecclesiastes 12:1 ISV*

Merlin was now stricken in age. At 60 years she was still dreaming. Not of becoming a medical doctor but of one day nursing her grandchildren. She was now hoping that her pension fund was enough to see her live a peaceful quiet old life. Like the scripture above tells us. Merlin had come to those troublesome days of her life. Remembering your creator in the scripture informs us that our lives must be lived in the way the creator intended. If you forsake your God-given dream, you will end up living in regret your whole life.

How do people end up like Merlin? Once innocent with pure childhood dreams to an old age of regret. What and where did it all go wrong? When and how did Merlin end up in the misery of unfulfilled dreams?

The systems of this world corrupted Merlin's childhood dream. The school she went to, the church she attended, her peers and the norms of the society she grew up in all made a great contribution to Merlin's plight.

The story of Merlin is by and large the experience of many people today. As you read this story ask yourself some critical questions that will help you not to end up like Merlin. Realize that your life is not on "PAUSE". Every day that passes by, I want you to know that you are moving closer to or far away from your God-given dream. Don't let your life waste away, take control.

## EMOTIONAL APOCALYPSE OF THOSE IN UNCLE SAM SLAVERY

Emotionally the person enslaved in Uncle Sam system goes through various experiences. The first feeling is that of despair as a person looks forward to getting a job. Just entering adulthood you feel a sense of the pressures of the burden of life. Meeting needs, getting married and raising a family, purchasing a house and all manner of demands begin to bring a sense of inadequacy on you. A burden of hopeless desperation pushes a person to the point where they care less about their true dreams, purpose and calling. The person is ready to do any job just to have a mental assurance of survival. In Most cases when people are in hopeless desperation, any form of employment will appease them.

When offered employment, a person will experience

the excitement that overcomes the hopelessness. There is an imagination of how all the pressures will be overthrown by the perceived might of a salary. As the payday draws close the excitement is just so escalated and the mind is filled with the possibilities the salary presents. This initial excitement is sustained for a while and then begins to wear off. A person will now enter into a phase of despondency as the imagined life of a salary that solves all challenges begins to get blurred. The motivation that enabled a person to get up every morning to go for work is lost and all that is left is disgruntled repetitious activities.

The commitment to work diminishes rapidly and various excuses of absence begin to be presented to the employers. This is the beginning of a long unpleasant journey through Uncle Sam system.

A study was done by the American Foundation for Suicide Prevention (AFSP), accessing the impact of the recent Great Recession which revealed that;

- The highest group in suicide rate was 45 to 64 years of age with 19.1% of 100,000 people in 2013.
- It was followed by 85 years and above with 18.6%
- Age 65 to 84 was third just ahead of age 25 to 44. Both had 16%

You will observe that the numbers of suicide prevalence increased with age. The older people have suffered so much at the hands of Uncle Sam; some can't hold it together, as a result, they take their lives.

The study revealed that people between the ages of

40 and 64 have had one of the lowest suicide rates but since 2007 the numbers seem to be defying the historical narrative. Recently baby boomers have had the highest rate of suicide of any age group in the United States.

Imagine the shock for those who had mortgages for houses that drastically lost market value in the recent Great Recession. That's the harsh reality for those dependent on Uncle Sam. Trapped in Uncle Sam system it is easy for a person to take their life. When hopelessness takes a hold, suicide becomes an easy escape option.

Many factors lead to workplace related suicides which include being laid off or being fired. Researchers discovered that men were 15 times more likely than women to kill themselves at work. It is believed that this is so because men seem to be under pressure as the breadwinners of their families.

Take for example those working in law enforcement's jobs. The temptation of suicide at work is more high, "when you have such easy access to a gun, suicide becomes an option" remarks Brian Fleming, a 32 year Boston Policy Office and instructor at the Boston Policy Academy. With the many stressors of working in Uncle Sam system, some are likely to go that gloomy path of self-murder.

The loss of a job or money due to poor financial decisions resulting from a lack of financial intelligence leads many to an emotional apocalypse. The lack of savings or social security, and chronic illness are things older adults usually experience, these factors can negatively impact their quality of life. Thus most people tend to resort to taking their own lives. People are pushed emotionally to the edge by the system they thought would free them.

Don't make the mistake of relying on Uncle Sam for your freedom. It is a depressing journey. If you are dependent on any system, when that system collapses you too will collapse.

## A FUTILE ATTEMPT TO MAKE SENSE OF UNCLE SAM SYSTEM

To overcome the despondency workers begin to seek for salary increments, revision of conditions of service and promotion opportunities. Labor unions are birthed out of this despondency but alas to say even the labor unions are a form of Uncle Sam system. This is an arrangement where people sell their voice to a few individuals who claim to speak for them. On the other hand, those seeking promotions go on to upgrade the professional qualifications and skills. *"Wage growth continued a longer-term trend of trailing behind productivity increases in most advanced economies, except during 2009, allowing companies to recover losses in profitability through lower wage increases"* (World Employment Social Outlook – 2015 Trends).

By wage freezes employers (companies and governments) maximize profits. Employers will not readily award increments just because you demand. When workers revolt employers only award a very minimal increment just to keep them quiet.

Consider these two scenarios below, though happening in different places they serve to educate us on the reality of results of a person's long stay in Uncle Sam system.

Firstly, a story is reported by the mobile giant company called Orange which was formally known as French Telecoms Company. The report highlighted that the company experienced 10 work-related suicide deaths. The company also reported a rash of self-inflicted deaths between 2008 and 2009.

Secondly, in Shenzhen China, the report at Foxconn said 18 workers attempted suicide in 2010 and in 2012 while another 150 workers threatened a mass death jump in protest of low wages and poor working conditions.

These are two different companies with a vast difference in culture, demography, economic conditions yet the same oppression of employment servitude. The employee's reactions are same because no matter the country, continent or company the system is the same.

We can observe that for Orange and Foxconn, workers resorted to desperate measure to express their displeasure at the system. Both industrial unrests and suicide kept increasing. People put so much hope and trust in a system they should be running away from. Those suicides are the final result of what people experience working for Uncle Sam.

Workers threatened mass death because they realized that they made more money for the company but only benefited peanuts in form of salary. Even that attempt didn't yield much because the only way to freedom is to stop working for Uncle Sam not to bargain for increment.

Increased wages and improved conditions of services is a song of futility. That song is not a freedom fighters song but a slave's hymn. These workers resorted to such action because their demands were not being addressed. Companies are not in business to enrich its employees but its owners and shareholders.

I want you to understand that physically, emotional,

socially Uncle Sam will take the best of you. You should watch out for the traps on the way of life. Most especially for Christians, you should begin to pattern your work life after the blueprint given by God in Eden. ***We need to find meaning and build a life worth living on a daily basis no matter our age.***

> *"Build your own dreams, or someone else will hire you to build theirs."*
> *(Farrah Gray)*

# CHAPTER 2
# GOLDEN POINTS

1. God made each man uniquely to be a solution to a problem in their generation but instead of pursuing that purpose people end up trapped in Uncle Sam system because of the desire to make a living.

2. The mindset of people in Uncle Sam system is that if they work harder and harder they will be able to earn enough to live free.

3. The spirit of bondage under Uncle Sam system brings people under a dark cloud of fear.

4. Living under Uncle Sam results in an unhealthy greed and appetite for more, people are led into a spending spree.

5. The only thing Uncle Sam system teaches you is how to spend money.

6. Under Uncle Sam, people will never be taught the laws of money; they will be earning a salary with no clue of how money works.

7. When in hopeless desperation, any form of employment will appease the individual.

## CHAPTER THREE

# UNCLE SAM'S BAIT

*"Too many people are thinking of security instead of opportunity. They seem more afraid of life than death"*
(James F. Bymes)

You are not living if you are not doing what you were born to do. You merely exist. Do you know the force that draws people away from their God-given work to merely working for a salary? Well, let's discuss this question.

As punishing as Uncle Sam system is, it's surprising that so many people still sell themselves into its bondage. It is amazing; people hardly make effort to seriously scrutinize the system. If you knew the reality of Uncle Sam's slavery would you be selling yourself out? Would you be among many people who just instinctively play along with the status quo? People who are always coming under compulsion to get employment so they could earn a salary. Working for Uncle Sam gives you a false sense of security while working in the place of your destiny presents opportunities for life fulfillment.

For every action there is an underlying motivation, thus when you seek to work for Uncle Sam, there is a motivation. All motions of waking up every morning and going for work are actions fueled by a powerful force. Negative or positive there is a motivation to every act. We should appreciate the fact that; work is not an end but a means to an end. For some, the job is a means for survival while for a few others it is a means for self-expression and destiny fulfillment. In this chapter, I want to consider what leads people to sell themselves into this wicked system of Uncle Sam.

People don't usually see the punishment of the system in broad, clear terms. The popular notion is that Uncle Sam's punishment is solely to due to an individual' causation. Believing this, people convince themselves that they will do better than those suffering at the hands of the system. Many are lured into the slavery of Uncle Sam because they are seeing some promise.

## BASIC HUMAN SURVIVAL INSTINCTS

Human beings have a basic instinct inclined to survival. We are always striving to meet needs of daily life. Psychologist Abraham Maslow in his publication; "motivation to work" gives us his theory of human motivation expressed in two categories of needs: deficiency and growth needs.

The deficiency needs are popularly called 'basic' needs while the growth needs are called 'being' needs. Maslow suggested that the first and most basic need humans have is the need for survival: that is, their physiological requirements for food, water, and shelter. People must have food to eat, water to drink, and a place to call home before they can think about anything else. Peradventure any of these physiological necessities is missing; people are motivated above all else to meet the missing need.

Growth needs; the need to know and understand, aesthetic needs and self-actualization needs, these needs can never be satisfied completely. Contrary to the deficiency needs, for which motivation diminishes when a need is satisfied, as growth needs are met, people's motivation to meet them increases.

Here is a list of Maslow's 7 types of human needs for you, beginning with the most basic.

1. Physiological needs.: cardinal to human life these needs express the need for survival, culminated in most basic needs of water, food, and shelter.

2. Safety and security needs.: this expresses firstly the feeling individuals get when they know no harm will befall them physically, mentally and emotionally. Secondly, the feeling people get in having a state of diminished anxiety.

3. Love and belongingness needs: known as social needs; love and belonging needs represent a feeling of being accepted by other people. Implies the experience of satisfaction derived from relating with others.

4. Self-worth and self-esteem needs. These needs express the positive feeling of self-value, the ability to foster a sense of pride in one's self. It includes the approval of others, self-respect , and freedom from embarrassment.

5. Need to know and understand: this is the need people have of making sense of the world around and within them.

6. Aesthetic needs: These needs refer to the quality of being creative, beautiful or artistically pleasing. It's the need for self-expression.

7. Self-actualization needs: an individual's needs

and desire to become everything he or she is capable of becoming. It is a question of personal full potential development.

Maslow suggested that individuals must meet the needs at the lower levels of his 'Hierarchy of needs' pyramid before they can successfully be motivated to tackle the next level's needs. The lowest four needs represent deficiency needs and the upper three levels represent growth needs.

Maslow proposed that if people grew up in an environment in which their needs are not meet, they will not be able to function in a healthy manner; as well-adjusted individuals.

For those who live under the dominance of the kingdom of God rather than the dominance of this world however, we know that the animalistic needs and desires of the flesh does not take priority over the essential needs of the soul. Jesus himself disputed this Maslow's theory in Matthew 4:4 when he said, *man shall not live by bread alone, but by every word that comes from the mouth of God.*

In this passage, we see that Jesus completely turns the Maslow's theory upon it's head. What Jesus is trying to tell us here is that whenever we put the physical material needs and desires over the soul and spiritual needs of the man, we come under the slavery bondage of the world's system. This world's system capitalizes on the physical and material needs of men, thereby using it to enslave them. But when we realize that the need to have relationship with God is paramount in the life of an individual, when we know that out of our relationship with God will come every other provision that we need, then we will stop seeking for material things above all other things. We would rather begin to live as the bible tells us to live. We begin to live by seeking first the kingdom of God and it's righteousness by which every other thing is added unto us.

When we put the relationship with the King of kings the author of the universe above every other relationship and needs, God becomes our provider. That is the order by which everything that is created in the world today was created. According to Genesis chapter 1, when there was nothing physical or material on the earth, there was the invisible God, who released from that invisible spiritual realm every physical and material thing that we see today.

The same shall be true for everyone of you my dear readers. If you will dare to believe God and put first the purpose for which he created you as the number one pursuit of your life. You will discover that every other thing shall be added unto you. Unfortunately, men are looking for a quick fix. We have forgotten that it is the invisible word that becomes flesh, the physical and material reality. When we then turn around the order of creation, we suffer the consequences.

This book is basically to reveal to us the evil consequences that we suffer when we put the pursuit of material, physical and financial goals as our primary pursuit in life. Our primary posit in life must be:

1. God, the advancement of his kingdom
2. The advancement of his kingdom on earth
3. Fulfillment of our calling and purpose on earth
4. Love and general well being to all men

When these values are exalted in our lifestyle above anything else, we discover abundance coming out of the right priority, such that we are able to fulfill all the needs that were enlisted in the pyramid of Maslow. In this case however we are free to pursue self-fulfillment. We are free to serve the creator of the universe. We are free to function on the earth as we are made to function, fulfilling our purpose and mission on the earth. By so doing, bringing glory and honor to the king of the universe.

Not knowing this above stated truth the uncle Sam psychological model supported by Maslow's doctrine is the basis on which most of today's ostensible life is patterned. Thus Uncle Sam (government, company owners and shareholder) highly value Maslow's theory. The theory is used to develop management practices and organization philosophies. Employers implement this theory through various strategies which include:

- Recognition of employee's accomplishment through awards, bonuses, promotion etc.
- Provision of financial security through monthly salary and pensions.
- Creation of a work environment that enables employees to socialize. For example, a research conducted by IBM showed that IBM held a *"family day"* picnic each spring near its Armonk, New York headquarters in order to foster a synergy of team spirit. This, in turn, brought about much collaboration among employees.
- Promotion of a healthy workforce. In a research

carried out by the Hershey Foods Corporation and Southern California, Edison Company showed that Employees are provided with insurance rebates with healthy lifestyles while extra premiums were given to those with risk habits like smoking.

Drawing strength from Maslow's theory of motivation, employers have gained mastery of the art of retaining its slaves. Employers know how to satisfy an individual enough to keep them in the job.

The promise of a regular income till death seems to be the solution for most people. A salary and social security are the best response Uncle Sam system offers to appease the needs of individuals and their families. This hierarchy defines the skeleton that holds Uncle Sam system together.

## THE MISSING LEVEL IN MASLOW'S HIERARCHY

For Christians; the foremost need is the greater need for the kingdom of God. Jesus Christ said,

> "Therefore take no thought, saying, What shall we eat? or, What shall we drink? or, Wherewithal shall we be clothed? (For after all these things do the Gentiles seek:) for your heavenly Father knoweth that ye have need of all these things. But seek ye first the kingdom of God, and his righteousness; and all these things shall be added unto you".
>
> *Matthew 6:33.*

As we see in this passage of scripture, if a person prior-itizes the kingdom of God and his righteousness, then he can rest in confidence that his needs will be provided for. The concept being established here is not that Christians should not work but only go to church. What is being established in this scripture is the motivation for work. Every Christian should operate by an extended Hier-archy of needs which places, the pursuit of the Kingdom of God and His righteousness at the base of the pyramid. The foremost motivation for work, therefore, must be working to expand the kingdom of God.

Living life by Maslow's hierarchy is the reason many people are led in Uncle Sam slavery. As you read this book, I hope you are realizing that when the pressure to survival (meet physiological needs) take control of your life, you will be willingly selling yourself out to Uncle Sam. Your food, your water and your shelter should be "the kingdom of God and His righteousness".

## THE DESIRE TO MAKE MONEY

Living in a world where people are celebrated for mate-rial possession, people are presented with the need and pressure to rise above their fellows in social standing by making material wealth acquisition their quest. Beloved, you must understand that it is through the desire for money that the world system enslaves people.

**"For the love of money is the root of all evil: which while some coveted after, they have erred from the faith, and pierced themselves through with many sorrows"**

*1Timothy 6:10*

The people of my country, Nigeria, are known for possessing a strong spirit of tenacity. We Nigerians possess a deep desire to 'make it' in life. I must say, this desire to succeed and be accomplished is not wrong in itself. Unfortunately when a person is motivated by survival, this desire can lead to very saddening developments.

Let me illustrate by the story of 7 Nigerian nationals arrested in the Philippines for Internet Fraud.

Hoping to make some easy money overseas, 7 Nigerian nationals set out for the Philippines. Posing as students and tourists the fraudulent clique got to the Philippines without any suspicion.

After the time of their arrest, the suspects were confirmed as being members of a well-organized international syndicate of bank hackers.

Upon reaching the Philippines they rented a house and began to befriend local Philippine girls, this was a well-calculated move to win the hearts of the girls and later to use them for their fraudulent scam.

Citing stringent banking regulations placed on foreigners the girls were then asked to open bank accounts to help these Nigerians with some transactions. The unsuspecting girls would go ahead with the genuine conviction of simply helping their alleged boyfriends. The team later used the accounts to gain access to other individual bank accounts using e-mail addresses. At the time of arrest, it is alleged that at one point a sum of $20 million was withdrawn from one of the banks in just a month.

Such are the unfortunate stories that have earned Nigerian nationals special scrutiny when entering other countries. There are countless stories of drug, human trafficking and many other evils, all result from the desire to be successful.

The desire to make money sponsors these vices. The words of Henry Ford come to mind as a good reminder, Mr. Ford said, *"If money is your hope for independence, you will never have it. The only real security that a man can have in this world is a reserve of knowledge, experience, and ability"*. There is more to life than money. Your life will be in disorder if you make money acquisition your goal in life. Many people are distressed, oppressed, depressed and stressed due to the love of money.

The love of money is exemplified by ambitions of having money at all cost; money is elevated to lord over people. It is an amazing phenomenon that millions of people worldwide still succumb to the pressure of working for Uncle Sam? The reason is that they are coveting more money.

Most people suffer not because they lack money but because people covet money and they cannot have enough. Money is not wrong in itself but what is wrong is that base desire to have money for survival and self-glorification. This desire is, unfortunately, the pinnacle of all pursuits in the worldly system and the main cause of crimes like robbery, murders, forgery and many other social evils.

You may remember in recent years the Bernie Madoff scam. Bernie Madoff; widely considered having a magic touch as an investor pulled off a $50 Million scam that shocked the money markets. People were bewildered at how the 70-year-old managed such a Ponzi scheme without being discovered earlier. A Ponzi scheme is a form of fraud in which belief in the success of a nonexistent enterprise is fostered by the payment of quick returns to the first investors from money invested by later investors. That was Madoff's specialty.

Under critical analysis it was observable that it was virtually impossible to have returns like Madoff reported, that should have been a major warning signal. The numbers were just too good. Instead of that being a warning sign, it was rather an attraction for a lot of investors.

The scam negatively impacted people and corporations alike; that is beside the impact on stocks overall. The exposure of fraud on a mammoth scale was also devastating to individuals who trusted Madoff with their fortunes. Apart from individuals, nonprofit organizations like Yeshiva University, who counted on Madoff's purported secret trading system to help operate its institutions were negatively impacted too.

Just some two weeks before the scam was uncovered it is reported that one private bank executive had placed a sum of $10 million from a client while another family had $100 million with Madoff. One Californian woman remembered how she'd lost everything with Madoff.

You would expect that a man of Madoff's age and caliber would have learned the value of honesty and good stewardship. It is the love of money that is responsible for engineering such heartbreaking evils like Ponzi schemes. When money masters a person they can do the unthinkable. The point here is that Money is a bad master and it reveals the worst in a man.

## THE BIGGEST INSTRU-MENT OF ENSLAVEMENT

Larry Roth says, "The debt and work cycle is an inge-nious tool of subjugation. Make people think they need all these things, then they must have a job, and they give up control of their lives". Larry Roth words are a mouth full, giving us a picture of how most people are lead into economic slavery. You have to understand that the desire to make money is the biggest instrument Satan uses to get people hooked on to his system. The desire to make money is what is causing you to sell every day, hour, minute and second of your life to Uncle Sam.

You are exchanging your God given freedoms and liberties just to satisfy your desire to make money. The Bible tells us that the god of this world system is mammon. When the desire to make money becomes your motivation, you are worshiping mammon. You come under the power and rule of mammon.

Having more money is a good thing and this should be the goal of every Christian. What is wrong is that base desire; to make more money to catch up with Uncle Sam's artificial lifestyle. In a later chapter, I discuss how having a lot of money should be your goal as a Christian.

After the completion of this book, you will be able to know how having a lot of money is good when it is divorced from the base desire of survival.

Each and everyday people are bombarded with vicious advertisements of all kinds. By so doing, the people are constantly being fed with the desire to make more money. You see latest cars on the market, and these are advertised as the means of building self-confidence and assertiveness. They tell you that an improved home appliance will answer all your problems. Uncle Sam is busy feeding people with the desire to have more and more money. The desire for more money is in the true analysis the desire to spend money. That's what every person seeking freedom from Uncle Sam system should flee from; the constant need and desire for money to spend.

## SALARY ON THE HOOK

So, Uncle Sam sets bait on his fishing rod. Many people will never see the slavery and bondage of the system but only the monetary benefit of working for Uncle Sam. The only thing people see before them is the benefit of salary. Thus the desire to make money shuts the caution senses that enable a person to carefully scrutinize his work conditions. The result is that people lose the opportunity to avoid oppressive deals like Uncle Sam. People's danger sensors are numbed due to the loudness of the appeal of making more money to meet needs.

In most cases, people believe that the solution to the need and desire to spend is to earn money through salary. People see working for Uncle Sam as a better and safer way to earn money. People have been accustomed to believe that the only way to earn money is by getting a regular job. Uncle Sam system sponsors the thought that without salaried work people will not be able to survival.

Do you realize that a salary is fixed and never proportional to the profits made by the company? A bonus may be awarded to you on increased output but it is in no way a reflection of the greater profits earned or the value you create for the company. Let me ask you; *"is the salary you receive, a true reflection of all the gifts, talents and potentials you possess?"* A salary is what summarizes the value the system places on a person. I want you to realize that salary is an undervaluing of your abilities. You are worth more than Uncle Sam is paying you. What you are truly worth to your employer is the total value you create through your job. Is your salary commensurable to the value you create at your workplace? This is why you must seek to outsmart the system or even better, stop working for Uncle Sam.

## THE PROMISE OF SOCIAL SECURITY

Apart from salary, people are presented with another form of enticement which appeals to their old age. The system promises monetary assistance when a person is unable to earn an income in retirement. This is also bait set before people to lure them into getting a job with Uncle Sam for all their productive life. This offer sounds like the most caring gesture a government can do for its citizens but you will see in a later chapter how social security is not the best retirement option available.

Like death and taxes, growing old is an inevitable eventuality that we all must face regardless of nationality, gender or social standing. The intricacies of how long and where a person lives are dependent upon the individual's health and money. The one thing we can say for sure is that it's not getting any easy or less expensive to live longer. It is obvious that the longer everyone lives, the more likely it is that they'll need someone to help take care of them.

It is estimated that about 70% of Americans who reach age 65 will need some form of long-term care and for an

average of three years. And for many people, social security seems to offer that financial security. This reality
makes people stay in employment in order to secure as
many funds as possible for social security benefits.

Let us look at an example of how Uncle Sam keeps
people trapped in employment looking forward to retirement.

The Polish government decided to increase the
national retirement age with the aim of creating a
more sustainable system of pensions. The World Bank
supported that decision by granting Poland a Development Policy Loan. Michal Baj, a director in the country's
Ministry of Finance said, *"Pension reform is one of the
most important reforms in Poland, implemented after
1989. It gives sustainability to the system of pensions,"*

The new retirement age is 67, and under the reforms
guarantees a higher pension for increasingly healthier
pensioners. Michal Baj further said every additional
year a person spent at work could result in a ten percent
increase in pension. Feeding into the same thought, a
University lecturer encouraged that the reasons people
should decide to work longer are that their pension will
go up with every year of professional activity.

Ironically, reactions to these regulations received
mixed feelings among the Polish. Anna Rybowska, a
bank employee aged 31, said she was not looking forward
to working longer but believed the new rules would ultimately benefit the country. Let's think about that for a
moment. If the regulations would *"ultimately benefit
the country"*, why would Anna hope not to work longer?

*"A pension is a safety net for the future which is
necessary in many cases, not everyone has children*

*some people have no one to rely on and many people do not think about securing their future now, so they will certainly need support,"* Anna remarked.

The longer you work for Uncle Sam system the more you contribute into your pension fund. But like Anna, a reasonable percentage of Polish workforce was not ready to work longer but rather desired to retire early. The remark expressed by Anna of people who do not have children to take care of them in old age shows us how people desire to secure pensions and social security funds thus keeping them enslaved to the system.

## HOW GOOD DESIRES CAN LEAD YOU INTO UNCLE SAM SLAVERY

In our desire to make more money and provide better living conditions for our families, we become slaves to our jobs and employers. Every person desires to provide the best life possible for those they love. The world system strives to keep people under the constant feeling of inadequacy; always needing more money to meet more needs.

Dear to most Christians is a belief system that pronounces the need for a good family and better life. This is good in itself but without realizing it, this desire for upholding family value systems can lead us to sell ourselves to Uncle Sam system. No matter what you provide for your family there will always be something bigger, better and nicer than what you are currently providing. The desire to buy a house, for example, could be a means of entering slavery if you rely on this world system of the mortgage. Am reminded of a response one accomplished blogger gave when he describes what he calls the *"greatest buyer's remorse"*. He says *"home-*

*ownership is good for a lot of people, but unless you're financially and emotionally ready and can make a commitment beyond a couple years, it's not something you should jump into".* The decision to buy a house changed his life. Our blogger learned lessons through it all that made him better. Now when there's something he wants to do that requires money or commitment, he asks himself what thing is truly important in his life at that time. If the need he has does not hit the top two or three things on his priority list, he concludes that it's not a good idea to pursue.

The things that always seem as a legitimate demand for our money or perhaps the need for getting a mortgage is not always as it seems. Uncle Sam will encourage you to go ahead to get a job so that you can afford loan and mortgage requirements thus enslaving you. You will feel the urge to get a job in order to become credit worthy. Beware of the seemingly legitimate demands. Never allow sentimentalism to precede your financial decisions.

## PRESSURE TO MARRY AND START A FAMILY

Furthermore, the world system is set up in such a way that young people in their early 20s come under enormous pressure to marry and start a family without paying attention to the responsibility of such a life.

In Chinese tradition, for example, the idea of getting married and having kids at an early age is deep rooted. In the past, young girls would marry in their teens while boys often married in their early 20s. Giving their parents grandkids has always been viewed as a major achievement in Chinese tradition. Even the great philosopher Mencius once stated: *"There are three forms of unfilial conduct, of which the worst is to have no descendants".*

Many young people upon leaving college or university are suddenly overwhelmed by pressure from their parents and society at large to marry. Apart from having huge student loans, young people are under pressure to marry to please society. This pressure is ubiquitous throughout Mainland China. According to the country's family planning policy, women who marry at the age of 23 and men at the age of 25 are regarded as entering a *"late marriage."*

Many people go into marriage without setting themselves free financially and as such, they are gripped, attached to the system just to maintain the daily family motions of rent, food, children education, medical fees etc. As you progress in family responsibility and the general needs of daily life you begin to see the need to work hard and hard. In some countries, people have got to do more than one job just to make enough for monthly expenses without realizing that salary will never be enough to meet all your needs late alone set you free financially.

# THE NEED FOR OPEN EYES

Let's conclude with social welfare analysis. The system may seem to show concern for the people by implementing a system of social welfare. The social welfare program is a composite of health care spending; education spending; cash retirement benefits; other government cash transfers such as unemployment insurance and the earned-income tax credit; and non-cash aid such as food stamps and public housing.

These too are crippling vices that deprive individual's independent thought. People lose the resolve to gain freedom from the system. The opening of eyes, therefore, entails the appreciation of the concept of self-reliance.

> *"Increased self-reliance will lead to an enhanced sense of self-achievement, a principal component of human wellbeing".*
> *(Robert Rector)*

Apart from looking to government for aid and assistance the eyes of people need to be opened to realize that work is not just about meeting needs. If not awakened to this fact people will end up falling for Uncle Sam's bait. All the advertising going on every platform exists primary to feed people. They aim to feed populaces with the desire to make more money to meet their needs. Therefore rid yourself of the base desire of working to make money for spending. Successful recognition of the bait spells avoidance. People must never allow themselves to be toyed around by a system that pays them little stipends and later asks them to return it by spending it on just meeting needs. It is only when people know, that they will desire freedom from Uncle Sam system. Therefore know the system and Stop working for Uncle Sam.

# CHAPTER 3
# GOLDEN POINTS

1. Many are lured into the slavery of Uncle Sam because they are seeing some promise.

2. Abraham Maslow's psychological model is the basis on which most of ostensible life is patterned.

3. Salary and social security are the best response Uncle Sam system offers to appease the need for survival.

4. Every Christian should operate by an extended Hierarchy of needs which place the pursuit of the Kingdom of God and His righteousness at the base of the pyramid.

5. People have been accustomed to believe that the only way to earn money is by getting a regular job.

6. A salary is what summarizes the value the system places on a person. A salary is an under-valuation of people's abilities; people are worth more.

7. In our desire to make more money and provide better living conditions for our families, we become slaves to our jobs and employers.

8. The world system strives to keep people under the feeling of inadequacy, always needing more money to meet more needs.

9. The reality is that salary will never be enough to meet all your needs let alone set you free financially.

CHAPTER FOUR

# RETIREMENT AND SOCIAL SECURITY

Retirement is like doomsday. It is an impending reality of a life of none usefulness. After having labored for many years people have to come to a realization that they are no longer useful to the system. People give all their life to the system and in retirement, they have to come to terms that it is over; they are useless, they have nothing to offer Uncle Sam. This is a time when a person has to be divorced from the system; usually, this happens when one has attained a determined age by the system.

In the National Basketball Association, the name Spencer Haywood will resound as one legend with a career, unlike many NBA players. He was the first teenage U.S. Olympic basketball player and the only pro to secure MVP and many other accolades to his name. He went on to become rich, earning substantially. Like many life's novices, Heywood thought he was ready when he was retiring. He recounts, "Looking back on the financial aspects, it was tough times". As said by another former NBA player, *"leaving pro basketball is like jumping off a cliff. When you start a new career, you assume an entirely different role, and you start over as someone else".*

Starting all over again when all you know is working for Uncle Sam is never easy. The system corrupts people financial and all they know is to earn and spend money. A person in retirement seldom has knowledge of how to make their money grow thus they spend all retirement funds within a short period of time. It is estimated that 60 percent of NBA players are broke or declare bankruptcy within five years of retirement.

The remarks by James Donaldson, director of the NBA retired players association are worth pondering, he says, *"Very few athletes are prepared when they go into the NBA, and even fewer are prepared when they come out"*. The athletes are never prepared going in and thus lack the discipline required to save and invest the money they earn. When time to exit comes, they are never prepared and they spend all their funds without replenishing, thinking they will get another bonus. This applies to most people in other fields of endeavors too.

Unfortunately many people start and work jobs without a clear retirement path. They only realize it when the sun is setting on them and it's too late. They resign from aspiring freedom from the system.

Truly for most people, retirement is like *"jumping off a cliff"*. And this, as I have said, is not restricted just to the world of sport but applies to all fields of life. Thus the lessons must be learned and mistakes avoided because you have only one life to live therefore live it well.

## THE STATE OF GLOBAL RETIREMENT READINESS

The reality is that rapid demographic changes worldwide spell the inevitability of government's continuation to withdraw from providing the sort of safety net in retirement that they were able to for previous generations.

Alex Wynaendts CEO at Aegon in the 2016 Aegon

Retirement Readiness Survey, say that, "there is still a long way to go before retirement readiness can be declared mission accomplished". The survey showed that:

- In many ways, change over the last five years in retirement readiness has not been as fast as hoped.
- There has only been a slight improvement globally in retirement preparedness since 2012.
- Improvements in retirement planning and saving that were observed decreased due to a world-view that dissociates personal responsibility to provide income in retirement from individuals.

As you can see, very few of those currently in employment consider themselves ready to retire at normal retirement age with sufficient savings to enjoy the ideal retirement dream. Fulfillment of retirement aspirations is never realized because of lack of sufficient retirement funds. Retirement aspirations include spending time with friends and family, traveling, taking up new hobbies, etc. and in the case of Christians this dream could include volunteering for missions and engagement in many other activities meant to grow the kingdom of God.

These facts clearly show us that many people are not ready to leave employment just yet. Many will retire to a life of financial inadequacy. The system does not provide financial literacy to help improve the retirement readiness.

Mostly the responsibility of planning and funding

retirement is placed on government and other agencies. Unfortunately, many people usually have an impaired judgment and crippled attitude that sees the government as the sole planner and funder for their retirement. Moreover, around the world, many workers are heavily dependent on government subsidies and handouts like social welfare and as such people take no personal responsibility to save enough to adequately fund their retirement.

## RESPONSIBILITY FOR RETIREMENT FUNDING

The question still remains, who should be responsible for funding retirement? During the survey by AEGON, respondents were asked about the extent to which they agree or disagree with statements about this responsibility.

- Responses garnering the highest level of agreement related to government intervention - either through social security (75 percent) or the government encouraging employers to automatically enroll workers in a retirement plan (75 percent).

- 71 percent of respondents expressed that it should be a more balanced approach in which individuals, employers, and governments all play an equal role.

- Fewer individuals (62 percent) agree that they should save themselves through private pensions and other investments.

These statistics clearly indicate that a lot of people

have been conditioned not to make decisions of their own regarding retirement. People largely rely on the system to decide for them.

Fewer people can easily brave the fear and risk to stop working for Uncle Sam. At the core of the problem is attitude and behavior value system regarding whose responsibility it is to plan and fund for retirement. Dependence on the system is a blinder to opportunity, an investment crippler. Thus people in the system see themselves as helpless dependents. People should take personal responsibility for planning, funding and grow their retirement monies.

Retirement plans are your responsibility. You have to be in control. Don't let Uncle Sam rule your life, take account of your days. You must take charge of your life; retire when you want and not when the system reduces you to non-usefulness.

> **"Teach us to keep account of our days so we may develop inner wisdom"**
>
> *Psalm 90:12 ISV*

## WORKING FOR UNCLE SAM IS MERELY POSTPONING THE INEVITABLE

People mostly sell themselves out to Uncle Sam because of fear and greed. They are afraid they won't meet their needs. The popular thinking is that in working for Uncle Sam they can live free of the burden of meeting needs by the salary they earn. For years a person never saves anything for investment from their work and retire to be dependent on a pension that is also an initiative of Uncle Sam system to ease the minds of those who would revolt from working for the system.

If you begin working for Uncle Sam planning to retire at the statutory age, you are merely postponing the inevitable. In retirement, a person working for Uncle Sam will still be faced with the same hardship of meeting needs and paying bills. Life for that person revolves around meeting needs, paying bills and then bargaining for an increment or promotion. In retirement there is no bargaining; based on your employer and person contribution the system determines how much you are to receive monthly. You don't have the power over the dispensation of the pension funds. Many people have had to pay great prices, make serious sacrifices for them to be free from Uncle Sam.

## SACRIFICE YOUR PRESENT TO BUY YOUR FUTURE

Let's talk about making sacrifices. Allow me to illustrate by telling this story of a couple. One couple (who call themselves "frugal weirdos") are gearing up to retire in 2017. They have a definite date for stopping work so they can carry on their dreams. The couple is planning and taking steps to set themselves free from Uncle Sam system by the age of 33. Their plan is to save 71% of their income. For sure that's great determination. 71% is a great price to pay in this consumer driven society. We can also observe that they have determined an amount to save every month. To achieve this they're very selective about what and when they buy.

Instead of getting a new set of furniture, most of their

home furniture was purchased second-hand. And for mobility; a "cosmetically challenged" Honda Odyssey minivan does the job.

When the modern woman is defined by shopping tendencies, the wife hasn't bought clothes for over a year. The sort of imperfections that come with frugal living are inevitable, and instead of letting it irritate them, it's something they've chosen to embrace.

There are six important lessons that we can learn from this couple:

1. They set a definite year for retirement. Instead of starting jobs like everybody else, they have a goal and mission as they earn their income.

2. They determined a percent of their income to save. The savings were not left to chance. Purposefully and deliberately thought out percent was set and they disciplined themselves to follow through with it.

3. They have a definite amount they want to raise before retirement. The equation is: the planned years of working in relation to the percent of income saving is equal to "total" investment fund.

4. Planned years of work + Percentage of income savings = Available Investment funds on retirement

5. They watched their spending habits. They are careful with how they spend their money. They were selective with what and when they buy.

6. They had to ignore other people's ridiculing comments. All they cared about is their goal of

retiring early and not about pleasing anyone.

7.  Employ a frugal lifestyle. They didn't deny them-
    selves what they required for a healthy comfort-
    able life but they were pennywise.

> *"The important thing is this: to be
> able to at any moment to sacrifice
> what we are for what we could be"*
> *(Maharishi Mahesh Yogi)*

## THE SQUEEZE OF UNCLE SAM

Uncle Sam's mission is to gain all by any and all means possible. All men are endowed with great resources that they must use to fulfill their God-ordained purpose. Sadly many people have sold all that great resource to Uncle Sam. Uncle Sam system takes a good grip on people never to let them go until all these resources are depleted. The system has mastered the art of drawing out all the potentials by promising that through hard work a person will live free, satisfied and fulfilled. ***"The tragedy of life is not that it ends so soon, but that we wait so long to begin it".*** What is far worse is that a lot of people don't even begin to live because they sell all their years to Uncle Sam.

One Lady recounts that during her HR career there had been employee sentiments citing "bad bosses". The underachievers generated complaints from their boss - as well as their teammates. Bosses ironically complained of their employees. What was so distressing is that, almost without exception, all these disquieted employees were talented, intelligent, capable and good people. Like

Thomas Edison says *"If we all did the things we are capable of doing we would literally astound ourselves".* People live below their God-given potential and it frustrates their true self. Workers complaints are generated by a feeling of wanting to be and do more than the status quo.

Uncle Sam's concern for your life is to squeeze out of you the juice of destiny for the system's benefit and not for your benefit. That is why you should be bent on outsmarting this cruel worldly system. All your dreams and plans for life will only be illusions when you reach retirement; no money to start doing them, and left with no strength to engage productively in the passion of your life. Retirement is such a horrifying thought because people realize that most of what they can do is just sit and wait for death.

At least even when people work for Uncle Sam they at least have something to look forward to every morning, even though they are not happy about the whole ordeal. In retirement, there is nothing to look forward to in the morning. There is literally nothing to energize and kick start each day for those that retire from the slavery of Uncle Sam having worked there the whole life. I wonder how many of you are really living. Unfortunately, most people merely exist.

> *"Every man dies. Not every man truly lives"*
> *(Braveheart – The Movie)*

## A GRAND EXAMPLE: THE REALITY OF THE AMERICAN DREAM IN RETIREMENT

At the heart of the American Dream is a belief that a person can succeed financially with hard work and determination only. But from popular stories, those that attained the American Dream were men and women who divorced the system to work in the area of their passion. Bill Gate and Steve jobs left the education system in college to convert great ideas into great realities. Oprah Winfrey abdicated her role in daytime TV to pursue opportunities with her cable network. She accomplished great things following her passion.

When it comes to the American Dream, it is dawning little by little that many will only experience it as a dream and not a reality; mere flashes of imaginations at the mental level. Economic factors have in recent years caused anxiety among the American work public as to how sustainable the social funds will be in years to come. Consider for example the following:

- Most people in America will have to work till they are about 68 to 70 years old to simply be able to get by. According to the Aegon, full retirement age to receive Social Security benefits had been 65 for many years. However, beginning with people born in 1938 or later, that age gradually increases until it reaches 67 for people born after 1959.

- According to findings from the Transamerica Center for Retirement Studies' 2015 survey of American workers, 65% of Baby Boomers expect to phase into retirement, by working past age 65.

- Transamerica Center for Retirement Studies' 2015 survey of American workers further indicates that 53% of Baby Boomers plan to work at least part-time in retirement. However, jobs may not be readily available for them.

- In 2012, a law was passed to permit U.S. federal employees to phase into retirement by shifting from full-time to part-time work and receive partial retirement benefits while continuing to accrue prorated future retirement benefits. In order to take advantage of the phased retirement program, workers must spend at least 10 percent of their time mentoring younger workers, thereby ensuring critical knowledge transfer. While the plan is seen as a best practice in encouraging phased retirement and has the potential to reach 2.5 million government employees, to date very few government agencies have chosen to make it available to their employees.

You will agree with me that in light of these realities the American dream is a mere mirage. You must realize that the system is made to ensure that you are depleted of all resources before declaring you redundant. Thus if a person is working hard to attain the American dream with retirement funds, they are mistaken.

*"Is Social Security a good retirement plan"?* Economics professor Antony Davies shows that Americans stand to earn significantly less and assume more risk with Social Security than other investment options.

According to Davies, taxpayers would be better off both in terms of financial security and return on investment by investing their money privately. Social security is extremely expensive, soon to be insolvent, and doesn't even offer taxpayers the most bang for their buck. For those reasons, Prof. Davies argues that it is time for the government to phase out Social Security. Davies' solution is that the government should honor its obligations to current retirees while giving Americans the freedom to invest their money as they see fit.

Uncle Sam system usually feeds people with the fear of lose of their money if invested in other areas, like Treasury bills, stocks etc. Even though other forms of investment would yield greater benefits, people are not ready to take that risk because of Uncle Sam sweet talk. Do you think the system cares for you so much that they are troubled by your years in retirement? The valuable money you contribute in your working life is used to make more money for the system and then throw your peanuts. The American Dream is farfetched for those employed by Uncle Sam system. The system will only pay you enough to just get by just like they did when you were in employment.

## DON'T WORK TO RETIRE UNCLE SAM'S WAY BUT RETIRE TO REFIRE YOURSELF INTO YOUR CALLING

Retirement is not supposed to be a gloomy doomsday. You can decide to stop working for Uncle Sam early on in life. While retirees from Uncle Sam are people who have no usefulness to the system you can retire full of life and potential to work for yourself in your God-given place of calling. Retirement should, therefore, be necessitated by the emergences of your calling. Retire while you are still full of life to serve God as opposed to waiting till you are old. Imagine a man whose calling is to bring the kingdom of God to the world of soccer, finds a job as an architect. It's obvious that when this man retires say at age six-eight, having worked for Uncle Sam; he can try to establish himself in his calling but his strength will be failing him. But if he purposed to be free from Uncle Sam at the outset, he could perhaps have worked for five years as an architect, raise some capital to invest and move on to play soccer or better establish soccer academies while money works for him.

> *"Do what you can, with what you have, where you are"*
> *(Theodore Roosevelt)*

Most soccer players have played the game and retire before age forty to pursue politics, business, and others to become a great philanthropist. Retire to refire yourself into your passion.

Liberia's George Weah with no ambiguity was a legend in his day. He was named FIFA World Best Football Player of the year in 1995, becoming the first African player to win the award. In 2004 Pele named George as one of FIFA's 100 greatest living players. These are just but a few of the many of George Weah's achievements in the world of football. George retired from football to pursue other passions of his life. Today he is celebrated as a politician, humanitarian (UNICEF Goodwill Ambassador) and philanthropist.

Likewise, a person should retire from Uncle Sam so as

to pursue the dream of his life. And by the dream of his life, I don't mean chasing after a mirage like the "American dream" which is a mere illusion created by Uncle Sam system to enslave the working masses. I mean going full time for the purpose God created you for, as Dr, Myles Munroe said, ***"Every human heart cries and yearns for the same thing: a chance to fulfill his or her own dreams and desires. Even the poorest man has a dream"***.

## A CLASSIC RETIREMENT EXAMPLE

Aged only 33 years a young lady braved the odds and freed herself from the job that restricted her free spirit. Anita Dhake left her job as a lawyer in Chicago to follow her passion for traveling.

When she graduated law school, she didn't feel like a lawyer. She went on and passed the bar and still felt nothing. She started working, and she remembered thinking, "Why in the world are they giving me so much money? I don't know anything!" It took her a long time for her to realize that most people really don't have any idea what they're doing on this earth. Like many people, she didn't put enough credence in her abilities and passions. Firstly the law practice wasn't paying her because she knew things. They were paying her for her life.

Dhake spent the first year at work paying off her student loan debt. As soon as the debt was gone, she determined to go for early retirement. Her mind was set, her plan was concise; she set a minimum target amount at $450,000 (which translates into about $1,500 a month in passive income). She blew past that: and went from having over $100,000 in student loan debt to having almost $700,000 saved.

She constantly felt pressured to put work above family, friends, sleep, vacations, and everything else. Due to the seemly comfortable salary at the time, she figured to be getting the better end of the deal, *"I realized I only have one life, and I'll never get it back"*.

Retiring at age 33? Now that's a classic exit from Uncle Sam system. Well, you might say she was a rich lawyer and could afford to retire early. If all that is required is a good pay then we should have seen fewer lawyers. The system wants you to think that it is impossible to retire early and follow after your dreams. But the reality is that Dhake reached her goal through a strategy that combined smart saving, savvy investing and thrifty life choices.

Guess what? You too can do it. And this book gives you the opportunity to begin again, to make your life a fulfilling journey of adventures untold.

The story of Anita is punctuated by carefully thought out, disciplined and consistent steps which replicate the six lessons given in an earlier story:

1. Setting a definite year for retirement.
2. Determining a percent of monthly income to save.
3. Having a definite amount to raise before retirement.
4. Planned years of work + Percent of income savings = Available Investment funds on retirement

5.  Watching spending habits.
6.  Ignoring other people's ridiculing comments.
7.  Employing a frugal lifestyle.

You must come to a realization that life is too precious to be wasted on mundane things like working for Uncle Sam. It is that realization that will launch you out of the system into your God-given calling. You have only one life to live and don't waste it working for Uncle Sam.

*"Stop living as if you have 500 years to live"*
*(Bill Gates)*

## IS IT ALL WORTH IT?

Having worked for Uncle Sam most of your productive life is what Uncle Sam offers worth it. Is social security compensation befitting the amount of sacrifice you are putting into the system? A person sacrifices his God-given assignment, his precious destiny, and family for what? You sacrifice the pleasure and enjoyment you would have been gaining from doing work that defines your hobby and passion all for Uncle Sam's peanuts. The system is structured so as to ensure that a person in it has no chance of ever finding freedom. If you are merely surviving while employed by Uncle Sam, is it rational to think that what you are contributing into the system will make your retirement comfortable?

## WORK TO LIVE FULFILLED AND NOT FOR PENSION FUND

Like Anita Dhake, the proper approach should be

to look at work as a stepping stone towards achieving freedom from the system. Retirement and social security should not be the goal. Don't start to work with a view of being in the system till retirement age stipulated by the system. You will be selling precious years to this cruel worldly system. By working in the place of your calling, you will get much more out of life compared to social security benefits. Fulfillment and satisfaction in life are only guaranteed to those who chose to live free from Uncle Sam. Happy are those who are not depending on the system to survive. Those who stop working for Uncle Sam have gained independence and they can, therefore, afford to pursue their God-given dreams.

> *"There are two things to aim at in life: first to get what you want, and after that to enjoy it"*
> *(Logan Pearsall Smith)*

# CHAPTER 4
# GOLDEN POINTS

1. People give all their life to the system and in retirement, they have to come to terms that it is over; they are useless, they have nothing to offer Uncle Sam.

2. Uncle Sam system takes a good grip on people never to let them go until all their God-given resources are depleted.

3. Retirement is not supposed to be a gloomy doomsday. You can decide to stop working for Uncle Sam early on in life.

4. A person sacrifices his God-given assignment, his precious destiny for what? Sacrificing the pleasure and enjoyment he would have been gaining from doing work that defines his hobby and passion all for Uncle Sam's peanuts.

5. Don't start to work with a view of being in the system till retirement age stipulated by the system.

## CHAPTER FIVE

# MORTGAGING YOUR CHILDREN TO UNCLE SAM

Education has existed for as long as man has existed. Though methods of education have evolved, education is not a new phenomenon. Older generations taught skills, values, and tactics of survival to younger generations. Thus precious survival knowledge was retained from generation to generation. Younger generations thrived on the experience of older generations. Education was achieved through storytelling, family discussion, and practical instruction. Thus through this critical passing on of essential knowledge, communities have continued to survive.

Children grow up learning from their parents. Thus if a parent makes poor financial decisions, the child will grow up with that poor financial decision baseline.

The Concise Oxford English Dictionary defines the word educate as, to "Give intellectual, moral and social instructions". We must understand that an individual's psychological structure is formed in early childhood hence the urgency to properly educate the next generation. Under this current system, children will grow up to labor for salary without realizing their God-given dream.

Disillusioned, bored and tired with school a boy asked his mother, why he needed to put so much effort and time into studying subjects that were irrelevant to real life. And without much thought, the mother responded,

"Because if you don't get good grades, you won't get into college". The boy went on to tell the mother that with a college education or not, He was going to be rich.

With a tone of concern, the mother said, "Son, if you don't graduate from college, you won't get a good job and how do you plan to get rich without a good job".

The boy began to cite examples of rich people like Bill Gates the Harvard dropout who went on to build Microsoft and became a millionaire in his 30s. The boy's reasoning was that the top richest people in America didn't become rich by college education rather by following their passion and dream.

This story illustrates a very vital point. Parents will teach their children only what they know. There are very few young people who can think independent and desire on their own accord to be free from Uncle Sam. The young people need an awakening. They need to be taught systematically and deliberately how to find their life calling.

> *"The whole art of teaching is only the art of awakening the natural curiosity of young minds for the purpose of satisfying it afterward".*
> *(Anatole France)*

## WHO IS TEACHING YOU?

It is important that you answer this question of who has been teaching you about money matters. Most of what you know about money has just been picked up from here and there. That kind of knowledge is called *"street knowledge"*. In whatever field of life, street knowledge won't take you far. With certainty, only expert knowledge will bring you into greatness.

Would you feel safe going to a hospital and the person attending to you just picked up a few medical books from the street and that's all the training he's got? I believe you would be very apprehensive about the whole experience. The same apprehension is what you should have when people who know little or nothing about the laws of money try to educate you or your children in money matters. Would you allow a novice to instruct you in the school of money? Money is one of the most crucial areas of life thus the need for systematic and deliberate education.

Money is a currency of life. Jesus said money demands worship just like the almighty God demands worship. Such an important subject should not be left to chance but should have a deliberate education journey for all that seek to serve God with whole their heart.

Robert Kiyosaki says, ***"One of the reasons the rich get richer, the poor get poorer, and the middle-class struggles in debt are because the subject of money is taught at home, not in school. Most of us learn about money from our parents. So what can a poor parent tell their child about money? They simply say "Stay in school and study hard".***

A child may graduate with excellent grades but with a poor financial programming and mindset. From childhood, many people have been conditioned to be slaves to the world system. They are educated to get a job, work hard and retire. Through this kind of advice, parents have mortgaged their children to Uncle Sam.

# PARENTS ARE ROLE MODELS FOR THEIR CHILDREN

Many parents world over are selling their children to Uncle Sam without knowing it. The parent that has no knowledge of Uncle Sam system and how to gain freedom from it will encourage his/her children to also prepare to enter Uncle Sam system unconsciously.

In modern day parenting the only thing parents know and pass on to their children is; go to school, study hard, get a job, marry, have children and retire. All this is preparation to sell a child into the bondage of Uncle Sam. Be determined and purpose that this knowledge you are getting will not only sponsor your freedom but that you will also pass on this liberating truth to your children.

Most adults have never had any systematic deliberate education in the laws of money and as such many have been trapped in Uncle Sam system.

Early on I mentioned of Mainland China concerning the pressure young people are under; to get married at an early age. Here is a story that illustrates this pressure.

Born in 1988 in Beijing, Rose shares the pressure she has faced from family. Her parents are constantly urging her to get a boyfriend; sometimes to the point where they become unreasonable. "I have totally no idea what they are thinking. It seems the only reason they introduce me to people is because they want me to get into a relationship". Traditionally many Chinese parents look at whether a person is from a good family and has a decent job or not, Rose's parents, on the other hand, don't seem to care about things like that. Thinking about all the sacrifices her parents have made for her, Rose found herself torn between two options either to please her parents and get married or wait to settle before considering marriage. Her refusal to marry early could be misconstrued for rebellion.

Rose like many Chinese young people may succumb. Such a young lady with great potential may succumb to the pressure and never find freedom financially or even work in her life calling. Many young ladies have forsaken their God-given dreams and calling just to be housewives.

## "GIVE TO CAESAR WHAT BELONGS TO CAESAR"

Children have often times observed the power of Uncle Sam system first hand though they cannot tell exactly what it is. They observe how their parents stress over work and the need to meet a list of never ending needs. What powerful force is it that makes dad and mom care less about spending time with them? Even the time children get to spend with parents is only soured by parent's mumblings about how they will find cash to clear this or that bill etc.

Observable are the levels of commitment parent's show in matters of kingdom versus working for Uncle Sam.

In most Christian settings, one day is set aside to celebrate and worship God in community fellowship. Uncle Sam's power is so intense that even that one day never gets the full commitment.

Allow me to illustrate this by a story

A little girl tells her dad, "Dad, this time around tell your boss, you won't be on call". The story behind that demand by the girl is that for 3 consecutive years the father has been promising to take her and the whole family to the city's commercial fair. But he always finds himself being on call at work. He has to be home waiting, in case duty calls. Sometimes the whole day is wasted just sitting home and waiting to be called for work. When other fathers are taking the time to spoil their children with fun at the fair, this particular dad has no time, because he has to *"give to Caesar what belongs to Caesar"*. Sadly, that's how a lot of parents surrender their family happiness just for the sake of a salary. They make money but lose the things that matter most to them.

## ACTIONS SPEAK LOUDER THAN WORDS

What a person does is more significant than their words. What parents do in relation to work and money become guideposts for their children. Early on in life people are taught through unguided learning that life is all about working for Uncle Sam. While growing up almost everyone is dreaming of working for Uncle Sam someday. From a young age, kids begin to desire the so-called 'white collar jobs'. They are never informed about passion and life calling. It's only a few people that raise their children to ever dream of being independent and free of Uncle Sam's dominion.

Usually, the people that raise their children to live free of Uncle Sam are those who have found freedom themselves. It is always difficult, almost impossible to teach what you have not mastered.

An estimated 3% of people on the entire planet have found freedom from Uncle Sam thus only a small percentage of people worldwide are exposed to the knowledge that can set them free from this worldly system. A parent's actions are his children's classroom. When parents tell their children about how much they love them, children are left to wonder because in action, the love parents mostly profess is sold to Uncle Sam.

## CHILDREN ARE TRAINABLE

It is often said that the mind of a child is a clear blackboard until people start writing on it. Children are trainable. They are easily trainable than adults. We have left children's financial literacy to people who are paid by Uncle Sam to enslave our children. We need to take responsibility for our children. We must purpose that what our children will know about work and money will be the truth as taught in the word of God.

They say, *"It is impossible to teach an old dog new tricks"*. If the education of freedom from Uncle Sam system starts early in life, we can be sure that a generation of people free from the dominion of this worldly system will emerge. Principle upon principle, kids must begin to learn to think of independence from dependence on Uncle Sam. Parents can be the pointers for their children; pointers towards a life of enjoyment in work over mere survival.

**"Train up a child in the way he should go: and when he is old, he will not depart from it"**

*Proverbs 22:6*

## WHAT SHOULD BE THE CONCERN OF EVERY PARENT?

God did not put the responsibility of raising children to school teachers or babysitters. That is why every parent must be bent on passing on a legacy to his children through education. Every parent should be concerned for their children; least they also end up in a miserable old age retirement full of regrets? Can anything be done for the younger generation? Because of parental love towards children, many parents can do anything possible to ensure that their children are provided for. Parents provide food, clothing, entertainment, academic education etc. but very few provide the accurate financial education. The priority of child education in regarding matters of work and money should receive the same attention that is attached to providing food, clothing, and housing.

The call is to every person reading this book to also pass it on to those with a prospective long future ahead of them.

If the reader has not yet read my book on the laws of money please check on the Internet or in your nearest book store for the book titled - **Money Won't Make You Rich** by Sunday Adelaja.

# CHAPTER 5
# GOLDEN POINTS

1. In whatever field of life, street knowledge won't take you far but expert knowledge will certainly bring you into greatness.

2. Money is the only currency of life that Jesus said demands worship just like the almighty God demands worship.

3. In modern day parenting all that parents know and pass on to their children is; go to school, work hard, get a job and marry, have children and retire thus selling them to Uncle Sam.

4. Usually, the people that raise their children to live free of Uncle Sam are those who have found freedom themselves.

5. Children are trainable

6. Parents can be the pointers for their children; pointers towards a life of enjoyment in work or mere survival.

7. God did not put the responsibility of raising children to school teachers or babysitters.

# PART II

## Work: God's View versus Uncle Sam's View

CHAPTER SIX

# WHO IS YOUR LORD?

Alfonso Montuori & Isabella Conti, From Power to Partnership: Creating the Future of Love, Work, and Community say that, *"When survival or mere subsistence is at stake, a society can focus only on the overwhelming needs of the moment, and questions of meaningful work and leisure are considered purely academic. But we believe that the world has enough wealth to move all around humanity above survival and subsistence".*

People are so predominated by what they can amass for themselves to foster a sense of security thus the wealth that can help millions is trapped among few people. Money is given supreme authority in people's lives. Most of what people do all day long is to satisfy their need to have more money.

Every Christian professes Jesus as their Lord. But what does it really mean? Proclaiming Jesus as Lord means we are able and ready without question to **"OBEY"** what he commands us to do when he commands us to do it.

Many Christians will confidently say that Jesus Christ is the Lord of their lives. But alas this is mere talk; the vivid reality is that their lives are sold to Uncle Sam system. Even though many Christians have the desire to serve God with their time, talents and gifts, they fail to give themselves fully because they are trapped in Uncle Sam system.

Let me share a story of a veterinary doctor to illustrate what it means to be free to serve the Lord.

Though raised in a Christian home, Kit Flowers never realized how his life's work could intersect with the ministry.

Kit and his wife Jan had been sensing a call of the Lord into ministry. Desiring to obey the Lord, Kit and Jan continued praying, asking God to show them the way.

Like many Christians out there, Kit faithfully tithed to his church from his salary. In pursuing the desire to serve God, Kit and his wife decided to also tithe from the gross salary of his veterinary practice.

After the decision to tithe, Kit got a letter from Christian Veterinary Mission. In the letter, Kit read about the story of a veterinarian who for years served as a missionary to the Masai people in Kenya.

Kit was reading about a man who had been using his profession to advance God's kingdom purposes until an auto accident claimed his life.

Kit realized that this was the answer to their prayer. Soon after, Kit and Jan decided to head to Kenya.

In Kenya they visited many villages, treating and praying for animals. As Kit worked, explaining his work to the local Masai, he shared his faith in the Lord Jesus Christ.

Within 5 years, six villages he had served weekly had banded together and formed a church.

From this story, we see that Kit Flowers obeyed the Lord and went to Kenya and there God used him to influence the Masai people with the kingdom message. God was able to use Kit because he had surrendered his profession to the Lordship of Christ. His profession ceased to be just a means of survival.

Jesus didn't call people who were just lazing around, Peter, Andrew, John and James were busying in the fishing profession when Jesus called them. Matthew was busy managing city accounts when Jesus called him. The disciples of Jesus were from a culture that understood that Jesus being Lord of their lives meant that he was their owner and that he had supreme authority over them.

Thus to say, Jesus is Lord implies that we understand and accept him to dictate the course of our lives.

Jesus is the savior of all Christians but not all Christians have made Christ Jesus the Lord of their lives. Many Christian's allegiances is to Uncle Sam and not the Lord Jesus Christ as they profess. If Jesus is Lord of your life it means He owns your life exclusively. But in reality, Jesus Christ is far from being the owner of your entire life. You have sold yourself to Uncle Sam. Most Christians will dismiss the idea that Jesus is not their Lord but if you check their activities you soon discover who is Lord in their lives. People spend all their best hours, productive efforts and intelligence to earning a salary as opposed to using them to do the work of God of making His kingdom manifest on the earth.

## WHEN JESUS IS LORD – THE STORY OF HANNAH SINGHOSE

Giving of one's self wholly to the service of God is a high price in this world dominated by Uncle Sam. The story of Hannah Singhose is extraordinarily inspiring.

Hannah knew God was calling her to go on a short-term mission.

Later, Hannah left her full-time job to travel half way

around the world without any guarantee of what exactly she would do, how long she would stay, or where to sleep?

Hannah had always been interested in missions. But, she was just working a regular job. She worked as public health nurse in Tiny Forks, Washington (population of 3,000). Hannah conducted vaccination clinics and well-baby clinics, treated communicable diseases, tended the sick, elderly, moms and babies, and also served as a school nurse."

In spite of the risks involved in being without a job, Hannah fulfilled her work obligations, raised the money, packed a footlocker and headed to Bangkok, Thailand. She went as a volunteer with an organization called **"World Concern"**.

She arrived at a temporary home near a refugee camp filled with thousands of Cambodians who had fled the "killing fields" and the notorious free-form massacres of dictator Pol Pot.

Hannah's presence and purpose were all about preserving and saving lives. In a bamboo shack with an openslat floor, she supervised a tuberculosis clinic.

She was confronted with various heartbreaking scenarios during her service. Children held out their hands for a daily handful of rice, dried fish and vegetable seeds to plant in their gardens. She says the women were so malnourished they couldn't conceive. Yet as nutrition improved, new babies made their debut in the hospital wards.

As she served the community, Hannah began to train nurses how to take temperatures, test vision and check for lice. Every day she earned her students' respect. They had reason to be grateful.

After completing her six-month stay, Hannah went home to her farm in Forks. Yet somehow the term "short-term commitment" didn't match her desire to do more. In the fall of 1981, she flew to Somalia to fill in as a cook.

In 1986 she went to Ethiopia, where life's cruelty stopped her cold. In a remote village, an eight-year-old girl had been bitten by a poisonous snake. There was no serum to be found, and the distant hospital had run out. Hannah ended up going to the hospital and transporting the girl's body to the family.

Hannah stopped at a market where the parents bought a piece of white chamois cloth to wrap their daughter for burial. Hannah felt so bad. What if they had the medicine they needed, the young girl would still be alive, Hannah reasoned. That **"if"** question is a trigger of a personal calling. Regardless of such disappointing episodes, Hannah had not been prevented from going to some of the world's neediest regions.

In 1987 she flew to Liberia to work as a nurse for nine months. A few years later she served in Romania and Alaska. Once back in Forks, she flew to Romania again.

We can observe in this story that Hannah had set herself free from the desire to make money. The kind of impact Hannah was making is something people living for survival and routine of meeting daily needs can never make.

Her desire was to please the one she had surrendered her life to. Hannah could go wherever and whenever the Lord impressed it on her heart. She had overcome the pressure of survival.

Hannah was engaging in the same activities of nursing but the purpose this time was all about preserving and saving life not salary. We see that Hannah had surrendered her profession to the Lord as a tool for His use. Hannah was not doing what she was doing for the money. She was doing it to please the Lord.

Through Hannah story, we can conclude that Jesus is Lord over a person's life if:

- A person is free from the pressure of meeting daily needs to work for God anywhere He sends.
- A person has overcome the desire to make money and thus being able to work even when there is no salary.
- A Person is not using their profession only as a means of making a living.
- A person has surrendered their profession as a tool God can use to advance His purposes on earth.

## SLAVES TO WHOM YOU YIELD YOURSELVES

**"Know ye not, that to whom ye yield yourselves servants to obey, his servants ye are to whom ye obey"**

*Romans 6:16 KJV*

The principle in this verse is that by obedience to the dictates of money we become slaves and by revolt or disobedience we gain freedom from being mastered by it. Christians world over have yielded themselves to the power of money to obey its dictates.

Money is the Lord in the lives of many people

including many professing Christians. Almost everyone working in any form of Uncle Sam system has yielded himself to the power of money. It's clear that Jesus is not in control of people's time or any other area of their life. The desire to make money is dictating its programs on a lot of people. People are not free to **"OBEY"** the Lord Jesus Christ.

People all over the world, Christians alike, wake up every morning to go to work not to glorify the Lord but to secure a salary at the end of the month. If you are working for money to survive then money is your lord. When Jesus Christ is the Lord of your life, work ceases to be a means of survival but a journey of destiny fulfillment.

Many Christians confronted with this truth will deny it, justifying themselves that everyone is living like that; saying that the world system is like that and they consequently resign from ever trying to get enlightened. To you who are saying it can't be done, I want to say in the words of this famous Chinese proverb that, *"The person who says it cannot be done should not interrupt the person who is doing it"*.

## MAMMON THE GOD BEHIND UNCLE SAM SYSTEM

If God told you to move to another country to go and minister his love to the people of that country like Hannah Singhose would you leave your job and go? How many out there are ready to obey the Lord Jesus Christ in such a moment. For the moment you even think about such an idea, the daily needs of survival are already talking you out of obedience. Jesus said it emphatically in Matthew 6:24; *"No man can serve two masters: for either he will hate the one, and love the other; or else he will hold to the one, and despise the other. Ye cannot serve God and mammon".* The basic truth is that either Jesus is the Lord of your life or He is not. If Christ is not Lord, then mammon is.

If you are motivated by money then money is your master and you have despised the Lord Jesus Christ. Ask yourself, *"What is the motivation that gets me going for that job?"* In the verse quoted; Matthew 6:24, Jesus qualifies money as having the power to "Lord". Behind the desire for money is the spirit of mammon and that's why every Christian should earnestly desire to be free from the power money. You are either serving God or money; duo submission is an impossible endeavor. Christians despise the Lord Jesus Christ when they fail to obey him due to the demand of meeting daily needs. This, unfortunately, is the true reality. Christians need to awake to this truth, that they are largely subjected to Uncle Sam and the spirit of mammon and not the Lord Jesus as they profess.

Our daily pursuits and preoccupations clearly define the object of our love either mammon or Jesus Christ. If you love God with all your heart, mind, body and strength then you will readily obey him when he bids you "come that I may send you forth to do my work for which I created you".

## WHEN THE "CALLED" SELL THEIR CALLING

Hannah Singhose brought a song of hope into communities around the globe because of her obedience to the call. Instead of saying, "I think I've done all I can," she asks, "What next, Lord?" she would not have touched so many lives if all she cared for was just her belly.

Too many people who are called by God to greatness to their generations are just wasting their lives working for Uncle Sam. Each person comes to this life with endowments that should be a blessing to humanity. Many great gifts and talents which could have been used to save families, communities, and nations, to transform society, to empty the kingdom of darkness and populate God's kingdom have wasted their lives running up and down, morning and night in Uncle Sam system just for survival. What a sad state of affairs.

- How is Jesus the Lord of your life if all you know and seek is a salary meant to meet your own needs?
- How is Jesus the Lord of your life when all your time and effort is for salary?

You are selling out your calling when all your time and effort is being given to work for a salary.

Lordship is the only term we can use to effectively demonstrate if really Jesus is supreme in the lives of all those who claim to be his followers. Is really Jesus Christ having the official power to make legal decisions and judgments in your life? Have you subjected your time, talents, gifts, intelligence, and energies to Jesus? An individual can only answer in the affirmative if he/she has gained freedom from Uncle Sam.

Strive by all means to be free from Uncle Sam then you will truly allow Jesus to be the Lord of your life. The anthem of every Christian should be in the words of Theodore Monod, *"None of self, and all of thee"*.

*O the bitter shame and sorrow,*
*That a time could ever be,*
*When I let the savior's pity*
*Plead in vain and proudly answered*
*"All of self, and none of thee!*
*All of self, and none of thee!"*

*Yet He found me; I beheld Him*
*Bleeding on the accursed tree,*
*Heard Him pray, "Forgive them, Father!"*
*And my wistful heart said faintly,*
*"Some of self, and some of thee!*
*Some of self, and some of thee!"*

*Day by day His tender mercy,*
*Healing, helping, full and free,*
*Sweet and strong, and ah! So patient,*
*Brought me lower, while I whispered,*
*"Less of self, and more of thee!*
*Less of self, and more of thee!"*

*Higher than the highest heavens,*
*Deeper than the deepest sea,*
*Lord, Thy love at last hath conquered;*
*Grant me now my supplication,*
*"None of self, and all of thee!,*
*None of self and all of thee!"*

All who profess Christ should take delight in obeying every one of his commands and leading. That is forsaking all, for his sake. We are to desire earnestly to please him more than anything in this world. That should be the pursuit of every believer. Not salary.

Jesus Christ cannot share jurisdiction with another, either he is Lord or he is not. There is no half lording over. Duo lordship cannot exist in matters of Christ and mammon. Every person must choose to let Christ or to let money lord over them. Who is the Lord of your life?

# CHAPTER 6
# GOLDEN POINTS

1.  Jesus is the savior of all Christians but not all Christians have made Christ Jesus the Lord of their lives.

2.  By obedience to the dictates of money we become slaves and by revolt or disobedience, we gain freedom from being mastered by it.

3.  Behind the desire for money is the spirit of mammon and that's why every Christian should earnestly desire to be free from the power of money.

4.  Jesus cannot share jurisdiction with another either he is Lord or he is not. There is no duo lording over.

5.  If you are working for money to survive then money is your lord.

6.  When Jesus Christ is the Lord of your life, work ceases to be a means of survival but a journey of destiny fulfillment.

## CHAPTER SEVEN

# ARE YOU A MASTER OR A SLAVE OF MONEY

So far we have seen that the modern slavery of Uncle Sam system is a cruel reality and people willingly sell themselves into this bondage. Beware of the money trap. We live in a world that celebrates people of affluence. With money, you can purchase many things that other people only dream about. Money enables us to obtain the necessary comforts and amenities of life. In this present materialistic day, people are constantly coming under the pressure to make as much money as they possibly can.

As much as money is an indispensable instrument of modern day economic life, we should never allow ourselves to come under its control. We must rather be in control of money.

Instead of you controlling money, money may be controlling you. Wise people master money, whereas other people often fall into the money trap by becoming slaves to money. You can live above Uncle Sam system if you become a master over money. The starting point is gaining knowledge. You must educate yourself enough to prevent yourself from falling into the evil hands of money.

## HOW CAN YOU KNOW IF YOU
## A SLAVE TO MONEY

A slave is defined as **"a person who is the legal property of another and is forced to obey"**. The Concise Oxford English Dictionary further defines a slave as **"a person who is excessively dependent upon or controlled by something or someone"**. We become slaves when we live for money instead of living for a purpose. We are created for something not just for earning money. People are not free to follow their passions and dreams because they are not in charge of their lives anymore. People are owned by a system and the people that sponsor their survival.

The desire to make money has taken over thus money has become master over people. You are a slave to money when the pursuit for money is what primarily defines your daily priorities. In most cases people are ready to dump relationships, purpose, and fulfillment because a stronger force is controlling them; that is the desire for money. Working for money is slavery. You are a slave when you give yourself to work for a salary and not for purpose. Those who became slaves to money are ready to even commit a crime. People tell lies and commit all manner of evil in order to get money. The bible warns us saying *"For the love of money is the root of all evil: which while some coveted after, they have erred from the faith, and pierced themselves through with many sorrows"* (1Timothy 6:10). The power of money in enslaving people is not just them going after it but also that when they have obtained a little of it, they instinctively go on to spend it all.

You are a slave to money if money is dictating what

you can or cannot afford. Let me illustrate the point with a story;

Andrew, like any young boy, always dreamed of his parents having a home where he could have his own room. He always complained about his little sister misplacing his toys and making a mess of the shared room.

One day Andrew went for a sleep over at a classmate's home. Upon arrival, Andrew's classmate Paul excused himself and his visitor from the living room. The two boys played themselves to sleep in Paul's room. When he returned home, Andrew could not stop talking about what a wonderful time he had at Paul's.

Andrew had questions for his Dad. He wanted to know why his family lived in that part of town when they could live in the nice neighborhood like Paul's family. Why couldn't they have a house big enough for him to have his own room? That and many other questions raced through his mind. Finally, Andrew mastered courage and asked his Father.

Dad took little Andy, sat him on his laps and then begun to explain their plight. He narrated how that their family could not afford all those luxuries. He explained that being a high school teacher he earned a little money, unlike Paul's father who was a chartered accountant.

Andrew went to bed sad that night. He realized that his family was, according to Dad's explanation, unfortunate.

The truth behind the story is that Andrew's father had not mastered money. He was a slave to money. Only slaves to money talk about being unable to afford something.

Another example: say, you enter a shop and desire to

purchase an item. When you can't afford a particular desired item, it is money that is making your decisions.

You may desire to send your children to a better school but if you are a slave to money, you can't decide which school rather money will decide for you. You may want to live in a good and safe neighborhood but the power to choose is not in your hands because you are a slave. Money is what is dictating what you can and cannot afford. The reality is that you are a slave being ruled by money. You should be in charge, you should decide what is suitable for purchase, if you are a master over money; you will know how to manage, rule and command money that it will come in your hand for any item deemed fit for purchase. In such a case it's not a question of whether you can afford it or not, but a question of when to make the purchase.

You are a slave to money if:

- The pursuit of money is what primarily defines your daily priorities.
- Money makes the decisions of what you can or cannot afford.
- You can do anything even if it is illegal just to make money.
- You have sorrow and feel sad when you don't have money.
- You are captivated by the love of money.
- Money is controlling your actions.

## BECOME MASTER OVER MONEY

A master is defined as a person who has other people working for him; thus being a master over money entails you being in total control of it that you are no longer working for money but money is working for you. Money won't solve all your problems but it will certainly solve many of them.

While others are ruled by money, being a master implies a person who has complete control over money. The reality is that regarding money there are many slaves than masters. Money is ruling millions of people while only a small percent of people have gained mastery of money.

You are a master over money if you are on top of it; your actions are no longer influenced by the desire to make more money or the fear of failure to meet needs. To be a master over money you need to set yourself free from the dictates of money. A sure sign of mastery of money is when you can look at money and are not dazed by its power. Masters rule and control; they are in charge of money through the knowledge and constant application of the laws of money. You are a master over money when you have so much money that you don't need to work for money rather money is now working for you.

You are a master over money if:

- Your actions are not influenced by the desire to make money.

- Your actions are not motivated by fear or failure to meet needs.

- You know the value of money and ways of managing and multiplying it.

- You have gained control over money through the knowledge and constant application of the laws of money.

- Money is working for you to bring more money for what you require.

## MINDSET CHANGE: A PREREQUISITE TO MASTERING MONEY

Becoming a master over money cannot be achieved without a rigorous mind renewing. As Benjamin Disraeli says, *"Nurture your mind with great thoughts, for you will never go any higher than you think"*. One must strive to gain the knowledge of the laws of money to be free from its influence. Mastery over money is crucial because if you are not in charge money will be running your life and you won't have the time to do what God created you to do. To be a master over money you need to learn the laws of money. Uncle Sam only teaches people how to spend money and never teaches them to save and invest.

Very few people if any pay attention to obtaining financial intelligence by educating themselves in the laws of money. If you are going to be a master over money, you need to break free from the mindset that led and has kept you trapped in Uncle Sam system. People spend money on snacks, beverages and on all sorts of things but never on materials that can bring them mastery over money. *"If a man empties his purse into his head, no man can take it away from him. An investment in knowledge always pays the best interest"*. Resolve to educate yourself in the laws of money and gain your freedom from Uncle Sam by becoming a master over money. In the world of oriental arts people spend years of training; body, soul, and spirit to become masters in a particular discipline. Likewise becoming a master over money will not happen overnight, one has to put effort to find the knowledge that will bring them into mastery.

## WHY YOU SHOULD BE A MASTER OVER MONEY

Why do Christians need to be masters over money? Beloved, **we need to master money and dominate it so that we can use it to serve God in our given purpose.** We should be masters over money so that we can use it to impose the kingdom of God over every sphere of life. This is the reason you need to be free from Uncle Sam. You must be free to serve your God anytime anywhere. Believers should become passionate about being free from Uncle Sam because it is cardinal to living a purposeful life. Every Christian should work towards gaining this freedom early on in life so that they don't have to be retired by Uncle Sam to serve God. When Christians are free from Uncle Sam they will like the Prophet Isaiah be able to say when God sought for a messenger; *"Also I heard the voice of the Lord, saying, Whom shall I send, and who will go for us? Then said I, Here am I; send me."* (Isaiah 6:8). Only those Christians who are free from the worldly system can say "Here am I, send me" for the power to make decisions is not left to money but is in their hands.

People have been wondering, asking why I am so confidently talking about going back to Africa to bring national and continental transformation. *"Leaving this big church you have built to go to Nigeria where things are hard?"* a logical question this might appear but for me when God says go, I say here am I, send me. I have set myself free from the grip of money. Thank God I have become a master over money and I can command it go and work for me. I command money to go bring more monies I require to fulfill my mandate. I am not dependent on any man or system for me to do the work of God; bringing the Kingdom to any and every sphere of life as God deems fit for me. Even the Church I have worked so hard to see blossom is not going to enslave me and keep me from **"OBEYING"** my Master. There are pastors out there whose churches have become a form of Uncle Sam which keeps them captivated.

We Christians need to master money so that:

- We can carry out the Great Commission. (Matthew 28:18-20). Our instructions then is to bring Christ to the people of the world, train them, and release them to change the world they come from.

- We are commanded to clothe, feed and house the needy and the poor. We need to be wealthy. We must be controlling money for us to do these things! (Matthew. 25:31-46)

- Our job is to manage and rule the earth for God. (Genesis 1:26 –28)

- It is good stewardship. Our ability to faithfully manage wealth produces in us godly qualities that shine to the glory of God. (Matt 25:14-34)

## MONEY IS A GOOD SLAVE BUT A BAD MASTER

Money is a good slave but a bad master. If you make money your slave, you will have the freedom to fulfill the purpose of God for your life. You will be able to command money as to what you want it to do for you. You will be able to obey your master; the Lord Jesus Christ without reservations. You will be working for purpose fulfillment, glorifying and honoring God anytime, everywhere. The stronghold of money over your life will be a thing of the past. You don't have to be among the many people out there working for money because of their need to survive. But if you let money get the best of you, you will always be running to and fro the earth and Satan loves it for God's people to be all over the place but never making any significant impact. Purpose it today, to be free from Uncle Sam by refusing to be enslaved by money. Work hard to become a master over it to the blessing of humanity and glory of God.

# CHAPTER 7
# GOLDEN POINTS

1. You are a slave to money when the pursuit for money is what primarily defines your daily priorities.

2. You are a slave when you give yourself to work and work not for a purpose but for survival. Working for money is slavery.

3. You are a master over money if you are on top of it; your actions are no longer influenced by the desire to make more money or the fear of failure to meet daily needs.

4. Becoming a master over money cannot be achieved without a rigorous mind renewal.

5. We need to master money and dominate it so that we can use it to serve God in our given purpose.

6. Money is a good slave but a bad master.

## CHAPTER EIGHT

# WORK SHOULD BE KINGDOM BUSINESS

*"Your work is going to fill a large part of your life, and the only way to be truly satisfied is to do what you believe is great work. And the only way to do great work is to love what you do"*
(Steve Jobs)

Everywhere you look in our world today, you can't help but notice pain, hurt, injustice, corruption and many other vices. What is the answer to the calamities of our world? With all our technological advances we seem not to know how to make this world a better place. We have been able to place a man on the moon yet we can't seem to find the key to world peace. In spite of all the religious calls for peace, G-8 and United Nations conferences the earth is still mingled with hunger, war, disease etc. Is there hope for our beloved earth?

*"The first thing man was given by his creator was a "kingdom". This initial assignment and mandate of "kingdom" is the creator's primary purpose and motivation for his creatures".*
(Dr. Myles Munroe)

The kingdom can be defined as "the government of a king". More specifically, a kingdom should be understood as the sovereign rulership and governing influence of a king over his territory, impacting that territory with his will, his culture, and his purpose. That impact is manifested in a culture and society reflecting the king's nature, values, and morals. In this discourse, the kingdom implies God's influence over a people, through his appointed ambassadors. We should understand that at the very heart of any kingdom is the heart of its king. Heaven in its entire expanse is infused with God's presence, character, and authority. That infusion is what earth needs, and through the kingdom mandate, Christians can manifest heaven's glories on earth. I propose to you that the kingdom of God is the answer to today's world problems.

One of the most important missions for a Christian is to spread the Kingdom of God on earth. God desires to use every believer to spread his kingdom everywhere in an outstanding manner. Therefore, whatever you do must all be contributing to the mission of spreading the Kingdom of God. It is through work that we can impact the earth with God's principles. In this chapter, we are going to examine the correct Christian understanding regarding work.

## YOU DON'T NEED TO ESCAPE EARTH TO EXPERIENCE HEAVEN

Unfortunately, many people want to leave earth and escape earth's troubles. If God wanted you in heaven he would have killed you the moment you gave your life to Jesus. Why do you want to go to heaven when God has not called for you? We don't have to escape from earth to enjoy the realities of heaven. You are a carrier of a kingdom; *"Neither shall they say, Lo here! or, lo there!*

*for, behold, the kingdom of God is within you"* (Luke 17:21). A man who realizes this truth no long works to earn a salary but through his work manifests God's kingdom. Don't preoccupy yourself with flying away to glory rather let your mind seek ways of manifesting heaven's glory on the earth.

## WORK: A MEANS FOR FULFILLING THE KINGDOM MANDATE

The prime preoccupation of every Christian should be the kingdom of God. The sole purpose of work should be to advance the kingdom of God in the sphere of life that God has placed you. You must understand that work is a means through which Christians fulfill the kingdom mandate. If you are working for a salary, you are surrendering your freedom to the dominion and power of Uncle Sam thus living below your kingdom mandate. You must understand that work is Kingdom business and not just a tool for earning money. Rather money is a tool with which you can accomplish God's purpose for which he created you. If the motive for your work is seeking the Kingdom of God then you are serving God in that sphere of influence he has placed you. Thus kingdom seekers must be motivated by purpose and not money.

Those who are seeking survival have exalted money to be the prime motivation. Every Christian can claim to be a sincere seeker of the Kingdom but only those who have set themselves free from the grip of money are truly kingdom seekers.

Just take a look at the social ills in your workplace, your neighborhood or country:

- Corruption
- Poverty
- Crime
- Prostitution
- Teenage pregnancy
- Abortion
- Street kids
- Money laundering
- Drug and alcohol abuse
- Divorce

These and many other social problems can only be answered if Christians begin to take the kingdom (government of God) into those areas. Christians should invade these spheres of life with the light of God and impose God's values. Let me ask you this; is your work allowing you to achieve this kingdom mandate?

Let us look at an example of how one Christian is carrying out this mandate.

Now a media mogul, Tyler Perry took his acting and movie making talents beyond the four walls of the church to revolutionize a whole industry.

While other talented actors just see the movie industry as a means to make huge monies, Tyler works to entertain and feed the spirit. There are always some surprising facets every time a new Tyler project is released.

Tyler Perry's Hollywood comedies are full of outspoken references to faith in God and the importance of family.

Regardless of being one of Hollywood accomplished individuals, Tyler has never lost touch with what first made him connect with his urban audience in Atlanta.

That quality that left the audience hungry and looking for more was his faith in Christ, which remains pronounced in his productions to date.

More than just a blend of hilarious characters and dramatic situations, Perry's unashamed embrace of the redeeming power of God and family has brought him from brokenness and poverty, and, as his movies show, he hasn't forgotten what he learned on his journey to the top.

And his movies are punctuated with those lessons. God rewards faithfulness. Today, Perry is one of Hollywood young successful and accomplished filmmakers.

What can you observe about Tyler's media career?

For Tyler Perry, prayer, faith, family values, and testimonies of God's redeeming power are the stories worth telling on the big screens.

Instead of these themes just ending up on Sunday morning services they are Saturday night premieres to Tyler Perry.

Tyler has turned the movie industry into a tool for propagating kingdom values and not just a money making machine.

The lesson to glean from Tyler Perry is that *"being a Christian in any industry presents an opportunity to influence that industry. Instead of conforming to the system, Christians should be transformers of worldly systems"*.

# IN PURSUIT OF THE KINGDOM

*"He is no fool who gives what he cannot keep to gain what he cannot lose"*
*(Jim Elliot)*

Dear reader to make the pursuit of the kingdom central in one's life is costly. If you are hoping for an easy way to the top in any industry, sorry I can't promise you that. You must know that if you go against the norms of the system then the journey might get abrasive. Imagine in an industry that promotes profanity, nudity, and other social corrupting values, Tyler Perry breaks through the film making industry with themes like the dignity of womanhood, prayer, faith and family values.

Following Tyler Perry's example, Christians must endeavor to promote kingdom values in their various walks of life without compromising. The temptation to incline to compromising standards is very high. But you must purpose to stand firm and glorify God. Don't go for gold but go for God.

# THE PRIORITY IS THE KINGDOM

**"But seek ye first the kingdom of God, and his righteousness; and all these things shall be added unto you"**

*Matthew 6:33*

The first purpose of work or employment is to bring the kingdom of God to dominate in the place of our work. The reign and rule of our God should be our first purpose in doing all work. The pursuit of all Christians, therefore, should become the establishment of cultures, values, and principles of the kingdom of God. You should desire to influence your work environment with godly character and not to work just to get a salary. To bring the righteousness of God should be your mission every day that you engage in work.

**"Thy kingdom come, Thy will be done on earth, as it is in heaven"**

*Matthew 6:10*

Here we can see that Jesus is establishing the believer's priorities in prayer. If the priority of prayer after fellowshipping with God is kingdom manifestation then it should also lead us to appreciate the fact that this priority should be number one on our daily schedules. You must understand that when the will of God is being done on earth then the kingdom of God is in manifestation. Above all else waking up every morning to engage in work is supposed to be for the advancement of the kingdom of God. We should sleep, eat, drink and work for the kingdom. This priority is crucial for destiny fulfillment.

If Christians are ever going to establish the influence and dominion of the kingdom of God they must set their priorities right. We must recognize that in the order of Christian priorities the kingdom comes above all else. *"But seek ye first the kingdom of God and his righteousness"*. This is the theme that you will see in all Tyler Perry's movies, plays, and books.

Unfortunately most Christians place '**God's Kingdom**'

at the self-actualization level of Maslow's hierarchy of needs. They have placed the pursuit of the kingdom of God and his righteousness at the top of the Pyramid instead of placing it at the base.

In the case of Tyler, he did not sell his ideas to some renowned Hollywood filmmakers but persevered through hard times. Disappointed at several startups yet determined, Perry had to work jobs unrelated to his passion while he revised his failed stage play. He staged the show also in several other cities, but disappointingly success still eluded him.

Broke, Perry was living out of his car for a period of time. "Can you imagine a six-foot-five man sleeping in a Geo Metro?" Perry was not overcome by the desire to meet basic needs in the Maslow's hierarchy. He pushed for his dream and he did attain.

Don't spend the best of your time, talents, and gifts just to acquire the basic needs. Sadly the little energy remaining is what you use to pursue matters of the kingdom. Jesus came to change that order. For those seeking to be free from Uncle Sam system, the kingdom of God is priority number one and not food, water or housing.

## CHRISTIANS ARE ASSIGNED TO SHINE LIGHT IN DARKNESS

Do you realize that this world is engulfed in gross darkness and in desperate need of light? Unfortunately, today's Christianity has restricted the shining of light to Sunday gathering of believers only. Not knowing that they are called to shine their light to those in darkness in the various places they go to for work.

Believers are not called to conform to but to transform their environment for God. That is, impacting the environment with the righteousness of God. When we enter into our places of work we should shine the righteousness of God thereby exposing all injustices and ills of this worldly system. We are the righteousness of God are agents of spreading His righteousness.

- Where are the Christians to enter into the dark world of politics and bring the light there?
- Where are the Christians to enter the world of media and flood the airwaves with God's love message?
- Where are the Christians who should be commanders of industries?
- Where are the Christians to educate our children?
- Where are the Christians to enter the world of science?

What is heartbreaking is that Christians have left the world of trade and industry, sports, media, and entertainment to non-Christians who are polluting this world with all manner of filth. Christians just sit and watch waiting for the rapture. It should not be so brethren. Rise up and turn your work into kingdom business.

## THE MASTER COMMANDED: "OCCUPY TILL I COME"

**"And he called his ten servants, and delivered them ten pounds, and said unto them, Occupy till I come"**

*Luke 19:13*

The Lord has ascended, waiting to obtain the fulfill consummation of the kingdom. But in the meanwhile, he left us a command; *"occupy till I come"*. We Christians are to be busy engaging in the business of the kingdom. Satan is working frantically to have God's children occupy themselves with activities that perpetuate the bondage of Uncle Sam in their lives.

We should be dominating the earth by spreading the flavor of the kingdom; peace, love, and joy. *"For the kingdom of God is not meat and drink; but righteousness, and peace, and joy in the Holy Ghost"*. (Romans 14:17).

We are kingdom carriers and the appearance of a Christian should be the end of misery, strife, and pain. Your appearance must be a decoration of righteousness, peace, joy, love, gentleness in every environment you enter.

The world of business, media, sports, education and other fields of life all need to be occupied by Christians. Christians should be commanders of industry and not slaves working themselves so hard just to survive. Imagine the revolution that you can bring to your work environment. Your obedience to fulfilling your kingdom mandate is the solution this world is waiting for. Stop working for a salary and begin to work for the expansion of the kingdom of God.

## THE GOAL OF ALL WORK IS THE KINGDOM

The goal of a person being self-employed or starting a corporation should be to advance the kingdom of God, which is to bring God's principles in that industry. Those in the world of finance, media, politics, sports, culture, and arts, industry etc. should realize that the goal is to saturate that sphere with the culture of the kingdom of God. When engaged in work the goal is *"thy kingdom come on earth as it is I heaven"*. Work is kingdom business. The only way work becomes kingdom business is when Christians get free from Uncle Sam system and are loosed from the power and grip of money.

> *"The only service you can render to God is to give expression to what he is trying to give the world, through you. The only service you can render to God is to make the very most of yourself in order that God may live in you to the utmost of your possibilities"*
> *(Wallace D.wattles)*

## KINGDOM-MINDEDNESS

What was Jesus primary message? If you carefully read the Bible you will agree that Jesus message was the message of the Kingdom and not any other message. Therefore if you desire to stop working for Uncle Sam then let the message of the Kingdom saturate your mind and affect your actions. We should be sold out for the advancement of Christ kingdom and his righteousness in the place of our vocation. Day in, day out, kingdom business should be constantly revolving in our minds by asking;

- How can I use my work to glorify my God?
- How can I spread the impact of the kingdom as I work?
- What is it that is in me that can bring a change in my work environment?

Beloved, we should have our mind set on things above; that is God's Kingdom. You should see heaven; a place of no sorrow, no pain, no tears and desire to see the same environment being replicated in the place of your work and endeavor. Your mind should constantly be thinking of, planning and devising methods of how best you can influence your environment for God.

## BECOMING A KINGDOM INFLUENCE

If you are going to be a person of influence then you must be set free from Uncle Sam system. Otherwise, the fear of being fired or demoted will always prevent you from standing up for the kingdom of God. Therefore to bring influence you must be free from the influence of Uncle Sam. If you are not free then no matter how much you are provoked by the evil happenings in your work environment you will be powerless to do anything about it.

Am sure you know that principles of kingdom righteousness are always resisted by the people of the world.

But if you are no longer under Uncle Sam's bondage you too can be resolute about your convictions and demand for and make the change. Christians should not dream of changing society if they continue to live under the influence of the world system. It is only when Christians set themselves free that they will assume the responsibility of being true ambassadors of the kingdom. They will become true ambassadors and agents of change on the earth.

To influence the system, you need to gain mastery of the rules and regulations that govern your industry then become a giant in that field.

Seeking and propagating the kingdom is living the way you were originally created to.

The lifestyle of a Christian should be to live the way they were originally created to, which is to seek and implement the kingdom of God and his righteousness on earth. To live for salary is to live far below your calling and purpose. Finding your calling is not that easy in this system which preconditions people for employment. Almost everyone goes through that phase of questioning trying to find their calling. The path to discovering your calling may not always be straightforward.

Christians are called to be rulers on the earth and they can only enter into this domain of rulership through self-emancipation. Your first priority must be spreading the kingdom of God. Uncle Sam teaches you to work for money and later spend it. When you gain freedom from the system your work becomes a tool to live for your purpose and fulfill your calling in life. The original life is for every Christian to live everyday for the sake of the kingdom. The passion must be to see God's will on earth. Seeing the kingdom manifested should be the fuel that drives your every action. Every believer should have an underlying proclivity towards the earth being filled with God's kingdom.

Allow me to conclude this chapter with the writings of Dr. Myles Munroe on the principle and concept of priority? He says priority is defined as:

- The principal thing.
- Putting first things first.
- Establishing the most important thing.
- Primary focus.
- Kingdom Principles
- Placing in order of importance.
- Placing highest value and worth upon.
- First among all others.

As we work our jobs we should thus have the kingdom of God as the highest priority. If our priorities determine the quality of life and dictate all of our actions and behavior, therefore it is essential that we understand and identify our priorities. We must understand that the greatest mistake in life is to be busy but not effective. The greatest failure is to be successful in the wrong assignment. You should realize that success is measured by the effective use of your time. Thus you cannot afford to waste another day working for Uncle Sam.

> *"The Miracle is not that we do his work, but that we are happy to do it"*
> *(Mother Teresa)*

# CHAPTER 8
# GOLDEN POINTS

1.  The purpose of work should be to advance the kingdom of God in the sphere of life that God has placed you.

2.  Work or employment is to bring the kingdom of God to dominate in the place of our work not to get a salary.

3.  When we enter in our places of work we should shine the righteousness of God thereby exposing all injustices and ills of this Uncle Sam dominated world.

4.  The only way work becomes kingdom business is when Christians get free from Uncle Sam system and are loosed from the power and grip of money.

5.  It is only when Christians set themselves free that they will assume the responsibility of being true ambassadors of the kingdom and agents of change on the earth.

6.  Every believer should have an underlying proclivity towards the earth being filled with God's kingdom.

CHAPTER NINE

# THE PURPOSE OF WORK IN GOD'S ECONOMY

In the world system, people work because they are in total and immediate dependence on salary to survive. As already highlighted, people's attitudes and actions are influenced strongly by the desire to earn money. When the subject of **"Stop working for Uncle Sam"** is under discussion, many people want to criticize it by saying God created man to work. They say encouraging people to stop working for Uncle Sam is promoting laziness. Unfortunately, they even misunderstand Paul's word when he says *"For even when we were with you, this we commanded you, that if any would not work, neither should he eat"*. (2 Thessalonians 3:10). This worldview is engineered by Uncle Sam system so as to keep people in perpetual bondage. In this chapter, I will introduce you to a correct biblical view of work. With this correct biblical view of work, you should be able to engage in hard work joyfully and purposefully.

## WHAT IS THE CORRECT VIEW OF WORK?

We must understand that work was created for man and not man for work. When men work like oxen; just being used by others for the benefit of having something to eat and wear, they are living below God's blueprint. Slavery kind of work is not the way God meant it to be. If work was made for man then work is supposed to serve a great purpose than just making a living.

## ADAM NEVER WORKED FOR SURVIVAL, WHY SHOULD YOU?

Surely God ordained work; God planted a garden and put the man in charge of it; to work and manage it. Careful scrutiny of this account in the book Genesis will reveal that work was not for survival because all that man needed for life was already provided for. The idea of work in God economy is not for survival but for the fulfillment of purpose.

You must know that work was instituted in the Garden of Eden where there was provision for all of the man's needs thus negating the idea of working for survival. Very few people realize that the emergence of surviving is not the reason for work in God's economy but it is in Uncle Sam system. The pressure of meeting needs was not the reason for Adam to till and cultivate the land.

Adam didn't work so that he could meet needs. He didn't work so that he could put a meal on the table. Do you know that Adam's daily food was already provided in the trees and herbs of the garden?

The garden scenario clearly depicts the right attitude towards work. The worldly system has successful mis-educated a lot of people into believing that work is meant for survival. In God's economy, work is a very different concept away from the worldly view of work. Do you understand exactly the creator's intent in giving you work? If you don't understand why God gave you work, you will not realize the need to stop working for Uncle Sam.

# WORK IS NOT PUNISHMENT FOR SIN

In most cases, people view work as God's punishment for humanity's shortcomings. That is why a lot of people consent to the slavery of Uncle Sam. As a matter of fact, the cruelty of Uncle Sam system has caused a lot of people to think that God is punishing them through work.

You will agree that this worldview encourages people to just hustle all their lifetime. By so doing people lose sight of their true calling in life. Unfortunately, most people have been convinced that work is a curse. They believe that by giving work to man God was punishing mankind for his sins. In most cases what is amplified in this world view is that God told the man that he will always sweat in order for the earth to yield benefit to him.

The underlying motivation in this world view is still the need to survive. The truth is that work was given to man before sin entered the world.

It is important for you to understand that work is not punishment or suffering for sin. Working for Uncle Sam, on the other hand, is punishment. It is a punishment that is self-inflicted and not God's curse. We should realize that the bondage of working for Uncle Sam is not fashioned by God. If we observe closely we will understand that what is punishing people and causing them pain and suffering in doing work is firstly the ignorance of Uncle Sam system and secondly the lack of required knowledge to set people free.

# WORK IS A BLESSING, NOT A CURSE

**"Jehovah will open unto thee his good treasure the heavens, to give the rain of thy land in its season, and to bless all the work of thy hand: and thou shalt lend unto many nations, and thou shalt not borrow"**

*Deuteronomy 28:12 - ASV*

This scripture shows us that God's blessings, e.g. rain, can only benefit us if our hands are engaged in some form of work. God's blessing can only manifest in your life through your work. Therefore through work, you can increase to become a lender and not a borrower.

Christians have been set free from the power of sin and the curse it brings. Thus correct mindset towards work is that work is a blessing from God not a punishment for sin. This is why among the many blessing you have received from God; work should be counted among them. Therefore, stopping to work for Uncle Sam is in no way a promotion of laziness rather it is a return to work as God planned it.

As a matter of fact throughout the scriptures, we observe that when we engage in work we inevitably put the blessing of God to work.

*"The blessing of the LORD, it maketh rich, and he addeth no sorrow with it"* (Proverbs 10:22). Again we observe in this scripture that man's enterprise is a means of actuating the blessing of God and it is not supposed to be a source of sorrow or pain. A man who truly understands this will work according to God's original intent

for creating work.

## WORK IS A TOOL FOR DESTINY FULFILLMENT AND AN EXPRESSION OF MAN'S DIVINE NATURE

I would also like for you to understand that in God's economy work is an expression of the God nature in you. As you express God's nature through work your life begins to be fulfilled and you find satisfaction in life. Every Christian knows that God is the creator. But do you know that God has given work to you so that through work you too can express the creative quality of God's nature in you? Man is made in the image of God therefore through work man expresses his creative quality.

You must realize that God's pleasure in creation is the reason why He instituted the blessing of work for humanity. You too could derive the same pleasure in doing work. You are not just supposed to work for a salary. Your work should bring you pleasure as you create products and service. The point I am stressing here is that "Work is a means for you to derive pleasure in life". As Mother Teresa says,

> *"There is always the danger that we may just do the work for the sake of the work. This is where the respect and the love and the devotion come in – that we do it to God, to Christ, and that's why we try to do it as beautifully as possible."*

> **"And God saw everything that he had made, and, behold, it was very good. And the evening and the morning were the sixth day".**
>
> *Genesis 1:31*

We can observe in this scripture given above that God did not look at His work in disgust but rather with pleasure. God saw that everything He created was good and that brought satisfaction to Him. Thus when we work we too should find the same satisfaction and enjoyment as God did in his work of creation. We should work in the spirit of excellence.

It is important for Christians to understand that working for Uncle Sam is never a source of satisfaction and enjoyment rather a source of agony. It should be fixed in our minds that work was not created for survival or as a means to earn a living. Rather as a means for you to fulfill your purpose and find pleasure and satisfaction.

A salary is only a compensation for your time and life at work.

> *"Let us more and more insist on raising funds of love, of kindness, of understanding, of peace. Money will come if we seek first the kingdom of God – the rest will be given".*
> *(Mother Teresa)*

Let me draw your attention to this question; should we not expect monetary rewards for our work? From our discussion so far we have established that work was not made for survival or salary but for expression of man's divine nature and pleasure. Should we then refuse an income? In God's economy, where a person is a master over money and not a slave, salary is only compensation and not the goal. If our work is to be meaningful we should understand that work is for the purpose, for self-fulfillment, and for your calling. As mother Teresa says, *"Money will come if we seek first the kingdom"*. Your salary does not matter when you are working according to God's original design.

On the other hand, because we serve a just God and we are still living in a world of injustice, you need to bargain for a good pay for your work even though the salary is not the motivation. You know your net worth, therefore, don't settle for peanuts just because you are a Christian working for a purpose.

The salary we earn while working temporary for Uncle Sam should be a means through which we set ourselves free from Uncle Sam's bondage. Understand that all forms of reward that come to us in the course of doing our work should never be elevated to the status of being primary. Rather should be seen as compensation for labor. The point here is that Salary, paycheck, promotions, bonuses, awards and all manner of motivation are therefore a reward for our engagement in Kingdom business, not the goal.

## WORK IS RENDERING SERVICE TO GOD

From earlier discussions, I gave a quote by Wallace D. Wattles which says that "the only service you can render to God is to give expression to what he is trying to give the world, through you. The only service you can render God is to make the very most of yourself in order that God may live in you to the utmost of your possibilities".

How do you give expression to what God is trying to give the world through you? The answer is, through work.

The right way for people to engage in work is that work should be principally a way of rendering service to God. Work should be a service to God, a way of establishing His kingdom on earth. I can never stress this point enough, in God's economy work is not for meeting your needs and those of your family. God says He will take care of your needs.

Work is a means for meeting the needs of the kingdom, and God is not unjust to fail to reward your kingdom enterprises. When you start a business or peradventure working for Uncle Sam in the meanwhile, you should regard it as service to God and not a livelihood. It is amazing to me to see so many people who are ignorant of the purpose of work. Through these truths, many people will come to a clear understanding thereby gaining freedom from Uncle Sam system. All work must, therefore, be a service to God and money is a byproduct of our service to God.

Those whose goal in work is salary and survival have not come to an accurate knowledge of what work is in God's economy. We, the redeemed are here on earth to show the qualities of our God. God is the creator and we too should be creators through our work. We should create brilliant and excellent second to none products and services for blessing humanity to the glory of God almighty.

> *"What you are is God's gift to you;*
> *what you become is your gift to God"*
> (Anthony Dalla Villa)

# CHAPTER 9
# GOLDEN POINTS

1. Work was created for man and not man for work.

2. The idea of work in God economy is not for survival but for the fulfillment of purpose.

3. Work is not punishment or suffering. It is Uncle Sam punishing people and not God.

4. But working for Uncle Sam system "maketh poor, and he addeth much sorrow with it"

5. When we work, we too should find the same satisfaction and enjoyment as God did in creating the universe.

6. Work should be a service to God, a way of establishing His kingdom on earth.

CHAPTER TEN

# IF YOU MUST WORK FOR UNCLE SAM

As we have seen through the stories of real people in earlier chapters who gained freedom by first working for Uncle Sam, lets us turn to those secrets of how we too can achieve that. Will you continue to just be a wage earner whose livelihood is completely dependent on the wage earned? Have you noticed that many people seem to live lives of desperation, striving to survive?

Your happiness, calling and purpose are put on hold because you are too busy in life's rat race. Meanwhile, life is passing you by.

How do you even begin to dream of stopping to work for Uncle Sam when you don't see how you can sustain yourself and family without the salary?

Let me ask you an important question at this stage:

Can you work for Uncle Sam system and yet be free from servitude?

Have you noticed in the stories I have given of people that are living free from Uncle Sam system that they started off by working for Uncle Sam? The point here is that they used the income they earned as a means towards self-emancipation. Remember the story of Anita Dhake the former Chicago-based lawyer. You too can find freedom and retire early still full strength to follow your calling. The key is the tripod strategy; smart saving, savvy investing, and thrifty life choices.

In this chapter, I will prove that there is a right way

a person can work under Uncle Sam and live free from the bondage. The idea being presented now may sound contradictory to what is in preceding chapters, but there is no contradiction whatsoever. Keep in mind that the title of the book is "stop working for Uncle Sam" and **not "never work for Uncle Sam".**

The goal in this book is to give you relevant help and not unrealistic fantasies. You must understand that we are talking about "stop working for Uncle Sam". But for most of you, temporal work in Uncle Sam system is required to make a smooth, mapped out exit once you have gained sufficient experience and saved up enough money.

## WHAT TO DO WHEN YOU HATE YOUR JOB

Let me share a story of a full-time Christian blogger to highlight some cardinal lessons of why we may need to work for Uncle Sam.

Bob spent about 5 years working at a Fortune 500 brokerage firm. Bob worked in three different departments and held 5 different titles over those 5 years. Regardless of those work placements something always felt out of place.

Bob began off with great ambition and enthusiasm just like everyone else. He expected that in a few years' time he would be sitting in his own pretty corner office.

Talking about the jobs he made Bob realize just how much he disliked his job. At the time, Bob didn't know that he wasn't working in his life's calling.

He has now realized that it was more of a preparation phase.

Bob says those 5 years were God's time-line for training, teaching and guiding him through that important challenging phase of life.

To sum up this story let's see what Bob did to survive those 5 years of a job he disliked. Firstly, he gave thanks to God on a daily basis for what he had even though the job was not his dream job.

Secondly, he worked even harder, believing that Christians must do all things to the glory of God.

And thirdly he prayed for favor with his superiors, the grace to endure the job and finally that God would show him to the right job for him.

We should observe the three cardinal lessons that Bob's story is highlighting for us, these should be part of our goal as we work for Uncle Sam temporarily.

- **Training:** Bob's work for Uncle Sam was God's means of training him for his promised land. Likewise, God will use our jobs to prepare us for the calling of our lives. Thus our attitude should not be that of laziness even if we are working for Uncle Sam. God is sharpening our skills and expanding our capacity so that we will be able to handle the giants in our promised land. As Malcolm X says, *"the future belongs to those who prepare for it today"*. Your future too must be prepared for. Use your today (current job) to prepare for your future (life calling).

- **Teaching:** The job you are doing today is a lesson for you to learn. Galileo Galilei says that *"you cannot teach a man anything; you can only help him find it within himself"*. You working for Uncle Sam serves the purpose of drawing out what is deep inside you as Proverbs 20:5 says *"Counsel in the heart of man is like deep water, but a man of understanding will draw it out".* Use your job to gain the understanding required for you to draw out all that God has loaded into you concerning your purpose and calling.

- **Guiding**: Your current job contains vital information that can point you to the path you need to take. It is an indicator to show you the way to your promised land. David Lloyd George says that "don't be afraid to take a big step if one is indicated; you cannot cross a chasm in two small steps". Working for Uncle Sam is just the start. Be ready to take the step when it is indicated and step out.

## A MESSAGE OF HOPE NOT CONDEMNATION

Do you know that the lack of knowledge about Uncle Sam system has led many people to enter Uncle Sam system and they have failed to come out of it? Unfortunately, a lot of people who are trapped in the system keep desiring freedom but have no idea how to gain their freedom. As a result, many of them resign from all efforts of ever setting themselves free.

The good news is that the wisdom principles I am presenting in this book hold the key to your emancipation.

This book is no way a condemnation of anyone working in Uncle Sam system but it is my heartfelt message of concern. My desire is to see the freedom of God's people from this modern form of slavery. You must attain your freedom so that you can serve God wholeheartedly without worrying about survival. Imagine yourself rich and free to serve God.

There is usually a tendency among people to criticize anything seemingly opposing their opinion. Instead of you justifying your work for Uncle Sam, please open your heart and mind to learn the right way. If you work in the right way, you will not only be free from Uncle Sam but you will be satisfied with your work, bring glory and honor to God. Others have done it before, you too, with a right attitude and commitment you can be free from Uncle Sam.

## CHRISTIANS ARE NOT TO SUFFER THE BURDEN OF WORRY FOR SURVIVAL

**"Therefore take no thought, saying, What shall we eat? or, What shall we drink? or, Wherewithal shall we be clothed? (For after all these things do the Gentiles seek:) for your heavenly Father knoweth that ye have need of all these things"**

*Matthew 6:29 – 33*

This scripture is clearly teaching us that Christians should not carry or suffer the burden of worry for survival. Understand that God assures you of daily bread if your prime concern becomes His kingdom and righteousness.

Society has conditioned people to think in terms of survival. But that is not the desire of God for His children. Rather Christians are supposed to be free from the world system so that they can influence it and manifest the Kingdom of God on the earth and propagate its dominion.

By operating the laws of money, Christians can be free from the dominion of Uncle Sam to serve their God. People have been enslaved for the fear of extinction. Evolutionary theory rules the minds of people as they strive daily for survival fearing the fateful extinction like those of ancient Mesozoic fossil reptiles. We are not dinosaurs living to survive from one day to another; but if you subject yourself to Uncle Sam you reduce yourself to that level of mere animal existence.

## LET UNCLE SAM PAY YOUR WAY INTO FREEDOM

*"Money frees you from doing things you dislike. Since I dislike doing nearly everything, money is handy."*
*(Groucho Marx)*

It is obvious that many people especially freshers in the workforce have no experience or income to stand without an initial source of income. You too may be at that point where you don't have sufficient funds to stop working for Uncle Sam. Getting a job is the first step for most people so that they could get the experience to stand on their own two feet.

Working for Uncle Sam is a first step to help you get the needed capital for you to begin working for yourself and go further to have money work for you.

The first way for you to rightly work for Uncle Sam is to purpose and plan to work in the system for only a few years with a view of saving up sufficient capital.

For instance, you can plan to work in the system for up to five years and from there on go on to put the money you have been saving into some investments.

While you are working for Uncle Sam, begin to educate your mind on possible investment options.

There is supposed to be a total divorcement of one's self from the survival mentality through knowledge of what work is in God's economy. You must abandon mere talk and wishes, set targets with regards to how much you will be saving monthly and be faithful to your resolutions.

The point here is that the purpose of working must be right even when you are working for Uncle Sam. Make money in Uncle Sam system which you can later invest to work for you while you have more time to pursue the goals and purposes of your life calling.

## LET YOUR HOBBY BECOME YOUR WORK

The second way a person can work in Uncle Sam and still be free from its bondage is by finding work that defines his passion. Make your hobby your work. If you are working just for the money and not because of passion and calling then you are still in bondage.

> *"When love and skills work together expect a masterpiece"*
> *(John Ruskin)*

The mistake most people make is to look for a job based on salary, instead of looking for work where they find fulfillment and purpose. Find your passion and go for it. Say for instance you love traveling, baking, counseling, swimming etc. then look for a job with those activities.

What makes a job right or wrong for you? The answer is "purpose" and not the remuneration. If the job is not involving your hobbies, watch out! It's a slave trap.

Remember, the purpose of work is man's expression of his God nature and in the process deriving pleasure. For example, if say your passion is football, you may not necessarily have to start a football club of your own right away. You could start by signing a contract with a football club and do the work you love. Play football and earn the money by the side.

You need to look for work that employs the use of your talents, gifts, and passions. Many people look for a job that carries a very attractive package. Don't make that mistake. As Marsha Sinetar says "do what you love and the money will follow" Don't let your career and professional endeavors be reduced to what you could get at the end of the month. There is no passion in the jobs a lot of people do hence instead of work being a source of joy it is a thorn in the flesh.

## TURN YOUR WORK INTO A PLEASURE CRUISE

Often time people think of work as a gloomy none entertaining venture hence there is no expectation of pleasure in doing work. *"Happiness lies in the joy of achievement and thrill of creative effort"*. You can turn you job into a pleasure cruise by being creative. The job you do should bring a feeling of happy satisfaction and enjoyment. Remember that *"success is not the key to happiness; happiness is the key to success"*.

Regrettable to note that the only enjoyment people gain from work these days are the salary they get and not in what they achieve through the work. Having made your hobby your work, make extra effort to turn that work into a pleasure cruise; a journey of never ending joy and delight. The radiance of such joy derived from doing the work that you love will always stand as a blessing to many of the people around you and you can take the opportunity to minister the love of God to them. "People are most satisfied with their jobs (and therefore most motivated) when those jobs give them the opportunity to experience achievement".

## WORK FOR EXPERIENCE NOT TO STAY

*"Experience is not what happens to a man. It is what a man does with what happens to him"*
*(Aldous Huxley)*

To effectively do the work of God for which you were created, you will need to get some experience. You need to understand how the world system operates because in carrying out your God-given assignment you will be in constant interaction with the system.

Uncle Sam system provides a training ground for you; get a job that equips you for your calling in life.

Daniel underwent three years of rigorous training in the Babylonian tongue,

> "And the king spake unto Ashpenaz the
> master of his eunuchs, that he should bring
> certain of the children of Israel, and of the
> king's seed, and of the princes; Children in
> whom was no blemish, but well favoured,
> and skilful in all wisdom, and cunning in
> knowledge, and understanding science, and
> such as had ability in them to stand in the
> king's palace, and whom they might teach the
> learning and the tongue of the Chaldeans"
>
> *Daniel 1:3 – 4*

We observe in the above scripture that for Daniel to be effective for his God in Babylon he needed to learn the ways of the Babylonians. We must know that experience is inevitable for an impactful living. Like Daniel, Uncle Sam is your Babylon. You too must get skillful insight if you are to be God's hero in the system.

If you lack experience you will be an embracement to your God and not a hero. Christians that rush into their sphere of influence assigned by God without preparation usually end up corrupted by the world system.

The scripture shows us that Daniel gained relevance in successive Babylonian governments because he combined his gifts with the experience he needed to interact with the system effectively. Daniel could stand before the king of Babylon and show forth the wonders of the kingdom of his God. If you too can combine or add to your gift and talents appropriate training, skills, and experience you will go on to be a person of influence that cannot be ignored or forgotten.

**"Meanwhile, Jesus kept on growing wiser and more mature, and in favor with God and his fellow man"**

*LUKE 2:52*

We can learn from the scripture that even Jesus had to grow up before he could set out into fulfilling his assignment. He was subjected to work in Joseph's workshop even though he was the savior of the world.

He learned very important social skills that would help him build a success ministry. He learned to be a judge of good character thus later in life he would know men for who they really were. You too are called to be a savior to a sphere of life but you must grow up. You need the experience for you to live an impactful life.

# CHAPTER 10
# GOLDEN POINTS

1.  Work temporary to raise required capital to work for yourself or even better make money work for you.

2.  Let Uncle Sam pay your way into freedom by investing the money you save while working in the system.

3.  Work in Uncle Sam system without being under the system's bondage by knowing and operating the Laws of money.

4.  Make your hobby, passion, gifts and talents to be your work.

5.  To rightly work for Uncle Sam you need to turn your work into pleasure

6.  Never enter Uncle Sam system to stay but work temporary to gain experience.

# PART III

## STRATEGIES AND WAYS TO SET YOUR-SELF FREE FROM UNCLE SAM SYSTEM

CHAPTER ELEVEN

# GET YOUR PRIORITIES RIGHT

To live effectively, you require an understanding of the principle and power of priorities. God limited your life on earth within the frame of time. Everything on earth is subject to time thus nobody can ignore time and be successful. This is why you must redeem your time from Uncle Sam.

Your destiny and life calling have a time limit. As Dean James says, ***"Dream as if you'll never die. Live as if you'll die today".*** Meaning that we are permitted to dream big but we should realize that every minute, hour, day, week, month and year counts in the realization of that dream. We should live to fulfill our dreams every moment. Our daily activities must be informed by what matters to us the most.

> *"How we spend our days is of course how we spend our lives"*
> *(Annie Dal-Lard)*

Time is the currency of life and if you mismanage it you have mismanaged your life. As a matter of fact, you don't have eternity to work on your life purpose and calling.

Your first step into freedom starts with setting your priorities right. You must understand that identifying the correct and right priority of life is the key to a successful and fulfilling life.

## WHAT MATTERS
## MOST TO YOU?

With regards to your time and life, you can't just do things in a disorganized, haphazard manner and expect to succeed. You must appreciate the fact that order is the beauty and serenity of life. Even the scripture confirms that God is not a God of confusion but of order. If you focus your energy and time on the minors of life, you become a minor in life. But if you focus on the majors, you will become a major.

It is important that you engage every day of your life with a sense of priority. Life can cheat you out of opportunities of greatness if you follow everything that seems good and legitimate.

The point here is that you must determine what is important to you and don't just flow with the motions.

What matters most to you? Is it your need to feed, have shelter, and be clothed or comfort? Having read this far you must have now refined your priorities. If you are ever going to live free you cannot afford to live haphazardly without any sense of priority.

Are God and His kingdom of first importance to you? Can people see the kingdom as being number one in your life by the way you spend your time? If you fail to establish correct and right priorities in your life, you will waste two most important human assets: your time and your energy. You will be wasting and spending life instead of living life.

When your priorities are not correct, you will find yourself busy with the wrong things. In most cases, you will be majoring on the minor. That is to say, you will be doing the unnecessary, or becoming preoccupied with the unimportant matters relating to your purpose and life calling.

Is the spread of the kingdom of foremost importance to you? If so, then you will resolve by all means to set yourself free from Uncle Sam system because without that freedom you won't succeed in bringing the kingdom to the sphere of your calling. You must determine at what level the pursuit of God's kingdom is on your priority list and make the necessary adjustment if it is not top.

## TOP ON YOUR PRIORITY LIST

By now you know that the first priority in work must be the establishment of the Kingdom of God and his righteousness. I have shown you that the purpose of work is to influence your workplace with kingdom culture and values. Therefore manifesting the Kingdom of God on earth (your sphere of influence) is "P1".

Enforcing Godly principals in every sector of life's endeavor should and must always be your chief goal for engaging in work. *"But seek ye first"*, not second, third or otherwise. Seeking the kingdom is supposed to be on the top of your priority list. Every other thing can come later. The kingdom must matter foremost over any other matter either food, clothing or housing and kid's education etc. Please understand that the kingdom must take precedence in your life.

Understanding this is the first and most important step in your quest to stop working for Uncle Sam. Prioritizing the Kingdom is *"the first key"* if you must stop working for Uncle Sam.

To work for the advancement of the kingdom of God must be the goal for your independence from this worldly system. If seeking the kingdom is not topping your priority list then you have not started your journey to stop working for Uncle Sam. First things must come first. If Christ's central goal and message were the kingdom then you too must make it your goal in your work.

## TAKING THE KINGDOM TO YOUR WORLD

Dear reader, do you know that wanting to do something and actually doing it are two different things. Planning alone is not enough. You must motivate yourself into implementing your desire to replicate God's kingdom in your workplace. You must convert your desire into real tangible action for it to be a blessing to humanity. To best illustrate this conversion of desire into practical steps let me share a story of Albert Pujols.

In the Sport's world, Albert Pujols is one of the best players in the MLB. You can't pitch around him because he's got such a long, searching swing. He routinely hits them into the corner and over the wall. From humble beginnings, he went from being a kid with a dream in the Dominican Republic, to playing professional baseball, Rookie of the Year, three National League MVPs, and winning two Gold Gloves and two World Championships!

He is quickly rising on the record charts. However, there's one thing that many people don't know and realize about him.

One thing about Albert is that he attributes all his accomplishments to God. Not crediting the success to himself but to the one he is living for, Christ Jesus.

How has Albert made the Kingdom mandate his primary goal in the game? Well, Albert says it doesn't matter if he hits a home run and it doesn't matter if his team wins a game and it doesn't matter if Albert goes four for four. Whatever happens at the end of the day, as long as I glorify His name, that's what it's all about. What matters is that Christ wins.

This is the most admirable thing about Pujols, all he does; he publicly attributes it all to Christ at a personal level.

You'll often hear a scantily clad singer at the Grammy's say "and I want to thank God!" But see their personal life; they live with no morals and without regard for God. Albert is different. And the fans love a hero.

We can see that with all this success, He knows that kids look at me with great admiration; he often meets kids telling him "Ah, you're my hero". His desire is to teach those kids. He tells them that God is the hero in his life. He shares to them how Jesus died on the cross for his sins, and how he wants to live the life of Christ.

Most people would give anything to be able to play baseball like Albert. Looking at his abilities and one can easily conclude that being a great baseball player is Albert's goal in life. As ridiculous as it might sound, Albert says baseball is not the chief ambition of his life. Becoming a great baseball player is not his primary focus. His life's goal is to bring glory to Jesus and not the Hall of Fame.

Instead of separating his professional life from his faith in God Albert talks about his faith proudly. The fact that this man, who is a national superstar, shares his faith at such a personal level shows you how strong his faith really is. Now that's taking the kingdom to the world of sport. Can you imagine the number of people he is reaching? They are for sure more than those in attendance of the average Church Sunday service.

## GLORIFYING GOD BY DOING KINGDOM BUSINESS

Many Christians believe that the most important thing in life is to give glory to God. And without dispute, that is definitely true. But very few understand what giving glory to God really means. We don't glorify God just by mere talk. Glorifying God is a matter of action. Let's take for example the ministry of Jesus Christ.

**"And great multitudes came unto him, having with them those that were lame, blind, dumb, maimed, and many others, and cast them down at Jesus' feet; and he healed them: Insomuch that the multitude wondered, when they saw the dumb to speak, the maimed to be whole, the lame to walk, and the blind to see: and they glorified the God of Israel".**

*Matthew 15:30 – 31*

We see that the acts of Jesus Christ were, in fact, the means by which God was glorified among the people.

When as a Doctor you go to your work with a radiance of God's love you are glorifying God. As a Lawyer when you gain freedom for those unjustly accused, you are glorifying God. Thus we shouldn't think of our work as being separate from our rendering glory to God.

Do you realize that when the kingdom of God takes

center stage in our workplace God is glorified? It is when we reveal God's nature in our immediacy that people rise to glorify our God. Therefore manifesting the kingdom is, in fact, the rendering of glory to God. You've got to get it right; you are not glorifying God if you place kingdom business secondary.

Jesus is our example of how we should live life. Just like Jesus, we must come to a place where we can say, *"My meat is to do the will of him that sent me and to finish his work"*, John 4:34. The scripture highlights to us that when Jesus preached, healed the sick, delivered the oppressed he was in actuality manifesting the kingdom of God. When he confronted the Pharisees, rebuked the scribes he was engaging in kingdom business. How does this apply to you and me?

It means that when you confront the wrongs at your workplace, expose corruption, renounce injustices or perhaps show God's love to an ostracized colleague in your office you are inexorably rendering glory to God. Therefore through work, we give glory to God.

The scripture is teaching us that, above all else, doing the will of God and actually finishing it must be our deepest desire. It must be the motivation for all of our actions.

## MAKING THE HEART OF GOD HAPPY BY DOING KINGDOM BUSINESS

It is the sincere desire and hope of almost every believer to one day appear before God and hear those wonderful words of commendation for a job well done.

> **"His lord said unto him, Well done, thou good and faithful servant…"**
>
> *Matthew 25:21*

This scripture shows us that we all have what it takes to fulfill God's mission of making the earth look like heaven. Every man has been given talents and gifts according to his/her ability. Every person is born to make history. God has placed talents, gifts, ideas etc. as means through which we should accomplish His mission.

God will only say, *"well done, thou good and faithful servant"* to those who are using the gifts and talents he has given them to glorify him by spreading his kingdom.

Can you confidently say that the work you are doing today is the best thing you can do to make the heart of God happy? Is the job you are doing the best way you could glorify God. Is the work you are doing what you were really created for?

To make the heart of God happy, you must be engaged in the work for which He created you. You are making God's heart happy when you engage in kingdom business because he created you to be an agent of his kingdom. You were created to reveal the realities of God's kingdom to that sphere of influence God as designated for you. The kingdom of God and his righteousness is P1.

## DESIRE TO BE FREE

After resolving your P1 which must be the kingdom of God and his righteousness, you need to inculcate in yourself a desire to be free from Uncle Sam system. You should never let the dream of being free die. As Langston

Hughes says, *"Hold fast to dreams, for if dreams die, life is a broken-winged bird that cannot fly"*. What you don't desire you cannot become. I know many of you reading this book are working for Uncle Sam. Please desire to be free.

The desire to be free will give birth to a quest for knowledge. Only knowledge of the truth will set you free. Understand that knowledge is only available to those who seek after it. If you seek you will find and if you search you will surely discover.

The more you get to know about the system and how to stop working for Uncle Sam the more the desire to be free will grow in you. There are people serving Uncle Sam who have resigned from ever trying to gain their freedom. As you read this book and revise the truth herein contend, may you never resign the efforts towards self-emancipation.

## PLAN AND ACT FOR YOUR FREEDOM

There is a popular slogan by an unknown author which says *"if you fail to plan, you plan to fail"*. This means that planning is the first step into success and lack of planning is choosing to fail. Do you know that it is one thing to have a desire and another to plan and act out your desire? Dreams fail because people fail to plan. Remember we are considering priorities. The scriptures tell us that *"Where there is no vision, the people perish"*, Proverbs 29:18. In most cases, people are perishing at the hands of Uncle Sam because they have not conceived a vision of their freedom. Yes, the desire to be free brings conception of a vision of a life free from the dominion of Uncle Sam. But where there is no plan people don't take action towards the vision and consequently perish in the final analysis. It is not enough to desire, you have to plan. There is a Japanese proverb that says, *"vision without action is a daydream. Action without vision is a nightmare"*. Thus to say, vision and action are sides of the same coin. You can't have one without the other and expect to succeed. At this moment you may need a paper and pen then answer the following questions:

1. **How much capital do you need to start your own venture**

Determine the amount of money required to give you a start in pursuing your own ventures of investment. For example, you could put a target amount of $100,000. This should be the amount that you raise while working for Uncle Sam. You need to conceive a mental picture of the required amount. If you don't set a target you won't have a milestone in your plan and you may end up continuing to be in bondage to the system your whole life.

From your regular salary, plan an amount that you will be saving. You can then grow your monthly percentage of saving steadily. Ideally, you want to be at a 50% savings of your salary till you reach your target. Now write out that exact amount on the piece of paper.

2. **How long will you work for the system to raise that capital?**

Charles Buxton says, *"You will never find time for anything. If you want time you must make it"*. If you are just hoping for a chance to appear for you to stop working for Uncle Sam then you are in for a long time of bondage. Sincerely speaking, you have to determine the time-frame for yourself. Based on your monthly saving you will be able to estimate a time frame for the period you need to work for the system. Thus the second item to write down on your piece of paper is the date of Exit from Uncle Sam.

### 3. How will you serve God as you work for the system?

Remember I earlier hinted that temporal work for Uncle Sam is there for the purpose of gaining experience and skills required for later work in your life calling. You should start implementing kingdom advancement strategies as you work for Uncle Sam. You don't have to just wait until you stop working for Uncle Sam to start minding kingdom business. Seek for ways in which you can manifest the kingdom of God as you go about your daily duties. The third element on your piece of paper should be a clear statement of how you are going to implement or bring the kingdom of God into your workplace.

### 4. What set of skills do you need to learn while working for the system?

I have elaborated that working temporary for Uncle Sam is a way for you to gain needed expertise to aid your work in the field of you calling. Therefore the goal in working for Uncle Sam is apprenticeship. Work in Uncle Sam to learn. Analyze your life, noting the skills and expertise that you have and those you lack. This brings you to the four component of your Exit plan. Write out the exact skills and competencies you must acquire before you stop working for Uncle Sam.

# TAKE THE DECISION

*"When you come to the edge of all the light you know and are about to step off into the darkness of the unknown, faith is knowing one of two things will happen: there will be something solid to stand on or you will be taught to fly"*

Dr. Martin Luther King Jr. said, ***"the time is always right to do what is right".*** Time to make and take that firm decision is today. You must take the decision. Decide now to start looking for ways and means to set yourself free from the dominion and lordship of Uncle Sam. That decision must be taken, if you don't take the decision and just wait for the opportunity, the opportunity will not come. Don't just sit and wait for a miracle, take the step. If you take that decision, God will bless that decision and you will see vividly your progression out of Uncle Sam's domineering hand. Let's look at a scripture to help illustrate this point:

> **"And there were four leprous men at the entering in of the gate: and they said one to another, Why sit we here until we die?"**
>
> *2 Kings 7:3*

The background to this verse is that the Syrian army had besieged Samaria, cutting it out from regional trade and as a result, there was a great famine in the land. These four lepers sat at the gate with options of either going back into the city, go to the Syrian camp or simply stay where they were. The four lepers choose to brave their fear and matched forward to the Syrian camp.

The verse above shows us that when people choose to merely sit and wait, they die. But when people choose to act, God backs their action. If you sit you die. It is time to make the decision and take that step. It is not until the four lepers moved that a miracle took place.

The step you take towards a hopeful future is what actuates the miracle in your life. God will not do for you what He has told and equipped you to do. The sound of the human steps you make towards freedom will be the power and thunder of the almighty God. Move and God will bless your effort.

Most Christians just sit and wait for things to happen by themselves or simply hoping God will make it happen. You must understand that the concept of waiting on God in the bible does not imply an absence of action. It accurately implies action dependent on God. When you operate life according to the principals set by God you are in retrospection waiting on God. Waiting on God means ceasing to do or live life your way or by your own terms. There is no more justification for your lack of action. You have to know what the bible says, know what you want and begin to live life.

In this chapter we have established the following:

First, that the Kingdom of God should take center stage in our work. The kingdom of God and His righteousness has to be P1.

Secondly, I have elaborated that you must conceive a desire to be free from Uncle Sam. Thirdly you must write out a clear plan of exit from Uncle Sam and don't leave it to chance. And lastly, I have emphasized the need for action. You must make the decision and take the step.

Life is predictable and by taking clear and concise steps you can be free from Uncle Sam.

For those of asking so what next? How do I get financially free if I resign? Again I want to remind you of the book I mentioned earlier titled Money won't make you rich. It will give you direction on which to go. I am presently working on another book that will help you with what to do when you are out of job. The book is called – why losing your job is the best thing that can happen to you. I hope to release it this year.

Another book that I am planning to release is – How to build a secure financial future. This book should also be available before the end of this year, so watch out and be on the look out for them.

# CHAPTER 10
# GOLDEN POINTS

1.  Setting priorities is the first step in gaining success and prosperity in all endeavors of life.

2.  Life can cheat you out of opportunities of greatness if you follow everything that seems good and legitimate.

3.  The first priority in work is the establishment of the Kingdom of God and his righteousness in the place of work; that is, to influence the workplace with kingdom culture and values.

4.  If Christ's central goal and message were the kingdom then you should make it your goal in your work.

5.  We don't glorify God just by mere talk; it is in action that we glorify God. When the kingdom takes center stage in our workplace God is glorified.

6.  To make the heart of God happy you must be engaged in the work for which He created you.

7.  It is one thing to desire and another to plan and act out your plan.

8.  But where there is no plan people don't take action towards vision and consequently perish in the final analysis

## CHAPTER TWELVE

# DISCOVER AND DEVELOP YOUR PASSION

*"The two most important days in your life are the day you are born and the day you find out why."*
*(Mark Twain)*

Robert Theobald says, **"Supposing we suddenly imagine, the world in which nearly everybody is doing what they want. Then we don't need to be paid in order to work and the whole issue of how money circulates, how we get things done, suddenly alters".** Your outlook on work will change drastically if you discover and start doing the work you are passionate about. Salary will cease to be the motivation any longer. In most cases, people rarely succeed doing work that is at variance with their core purpose and life calling. It is true when Dale Carnegie says that **"people rarely succeed unless they have fun in what they are doing".** If you are not enjoying your work you won't make the success.

After getting your priorities straightened, the next step is to discover what your passion is. You cannot define your life without knowing your passion and calling. You do not just merely exist. Each person is born with a calling. The discovery of that calling for your life is what sets you on a journey to your freedom from the bondage of Uncle Sam.

People live aimlessly achieving nothing because their

lives are not controlled by a definite passion. We are not to live life on trial basis, life is too precious to toy with. Leave experiments to science in laboratories and don't experiment with life. Mistakes in experimenting with life can be costly. I propose to you that the easiest way a person can stop working for Uncle Sam is by discovering his/her passion and calling.

An expert business coach says looking for career clues in one's choice of hobbies, interests, and vocational activities will provide the most fruitful direction for highly successful career choices. *"In fact, the earlier we are able to observe our personal tastes as they show up in hobbies and outside activities, the more powerful a lead these things will provide in steering us to meaningful professional and career choices."*

## THE PASSION DISCOVERY QUESTION

To discover your passion you must ask yourself this question, "what activity (work) would I do even if I am not paid?" Unless you answer that question your work will be a meaningless monotonous and frustrating experience. When you are working for your purpose and calling money ceases to be the motivation for work. Therefore discover what you love doing the most. That thing you can do even if there is no monetary compensation.

*"The one thing that you have that nobody else has is you. Your voice, your mind, your story, your vision. So write and draw and build and play and dance and live as only you can."*
*(Neil Gaiman)*

DISCOVER AND DEVELOP YOUR PASSION ■ 189

Implying that you are unique and specifically tailored made to do what no other human can do the way you would do it. And once you discover that uniqueness you will want to employ it even when there is no monetary reward.

## YOUR PASSION CAN TRANS-FORM THE WORLD

Engagement of your passion in work can bring about world transformation. If not global it will at least bring transformation in your world, which is your place of immediacy. You can transform your world if you follow after your passion and calling.  Making impact in life demands that you operate in the place of your calling else you will be second best trying to be someone you are not.

> *"You can have everything in life you want if you'll just help enough other people get what they want"*
> *(Zig Ziglar)*

You must see and determine how you can help people around you. You must go all-out to look for ways you could be a blessing to humanity with your calling. For example; if comedy is your calling and passion, you don't have to wait to enter Hollywood to change someone's life. You could start by bringing a smile to those individuals in the place of proximity; at your home, community, and office etc.

We have few people today who care to make a difference in their world. Lamentable to say that people would rather watch, complain and condemn but never stand up to take action that brings a difference. Your passion can make a big difference. As Harold Whiteman says, *"don't ask yourself what the world needs; ask yourself what makes you alive. And then go and do that. Because what the world needs is people who have come alive"*.

The question is; what is it that makes you alive?

## THE INEVITABILITY OF PASSION

Passion is an inevitable factor in the journey of life. Passion is defined as a strong and barely controllable emotion; it is an intense enthusiasm for something. Do you know that *"a man can succeed at almost anything for which he has unlimited enthusiasm"*? As Ralph Waldo Emerson puts it, *"Enthusiasm is the mother of effort, and without it, nothing great was ever achieved"*.

Consider the soccer icon, Lionel Messi's face of satisfaction and pleasure with each kick of the football. It is the passion that drives him beyond challenges of the game. That passion has enabled him to become a winner of FIFA's player of the year award five times. Passion has enabled him to endure painstaking training sessions that have developed excellent skills and mastery to become one of soccer's highest-paid players.

Passion makes people forget about the crowd and the need for keeping up appearances when engaged in their passion. What makes people brave the cold, heat and many other elements and circumstances to engage in their hobbies and their work is passion.

Passion should lead you to work. In most cases, people pursue careers and work engagements that are at variance with their passion thereby robbing themselves of the opportunity to work for purpose. As a result, they derive no pleasure in what they do; constantly subjected to the dominion of Uncle Sam.

Discovery of passion will set you on the right career path, therefore, you need to make every effort in discovering your passion. Let me share with you the fascinating story of Manny Pacquiao.

Seen as a symbol of success, modesty and professionalism Manny is one of the best athletes in the world today and a celebrated Hero of his country.

Growing up, Manny had to overcome a lot of heart-breaking challenges. Manny Pacquiao dropped out of elementary school and helped his mom by selling bread and homemade doughnuts peddling the streets of General Santos City. Going about with the sales Manny would be seen visiting other nearby villages and towns to compete in boxing matches in which he earned a little around $2. With this money, he would help his mom to meet their living expenses.

His family was so poor that at one time his father had to kill his pet dog for dinner. That experience would greatly impact young Manny's life. Bitter towards his father, Pacquiao ran away from home, wandering the street he slept on cardboard boxes to brave the cold nights.

With his passion for boxing, Manny still went on and moved to Manila where he continued to train and fight in matches even though he never earned much to see himself out of poverty.

Manny soon got a job at a local gym doing gardening, cleaning, and construction just to get by. Passionate about boxing he trained at the slightest chance he got. He trained passionately all day and all night when possible.

Usually, he would wake up the earliest and leave the gym at the latest possible time.

His passion for boxing enabled him to overcome people's stereotyping to achieve success. Several boxing promoters in his early days told him he was too small to be a boxer, a remark that would have caused many other people to give up.

To overcome that obstacle he would put rocks in his pockets for weighings so as to grow his stamina.

Regardless of besetting remarks passion for boxing drove Manny past those sentiments as he trained hard and vigorously to overcome what people said of him.

Manny Pacquiao hails his maternal uncle, Sardo Mejia as a hero who recognized the talent in him and introduced him to boxing. Watching a boxing match with his uncle one time, Manny says the Mike Tyson's defeat to James "Buster" Douglas in 1990 was an experience that changed his life.

Manny Pacquiao entered professional boxing at age 17 earning $2 per fight and in 1998 at age 19 he won the WBC flyweight belt in Thailand.

Today as you enter Manny Pacquiao's house, you are greeted by a display of world title trophies at various boxing categories; flyweight, super bantam-weight, featherweight, super featherweight, lightweight, welter-weight, and light middleweight.

Manny Pacquiao says his formula for success is dedication, perseverance, courage, extreme self-discipline, and prayer. Manny says

> *"Anyone will succeed in whatever field of endeavor in life by acquiring the same virtues and character that boxing world champions do"*

Manny's story helps us to see that no matter a person's family background, childhood experience, city or country of residence anyone can win in life. The key to winning in life is following passion. As Bruce Barton says, "Nothing splendid has ever been achieved except by those who dared believe that something inside of them was superior to circumstance."

## PASSION IS NOT FAR FETCHED

> "It's a funny thing about life; if you refuse to accept anything but the best – you very often get it"
> (W. Somerset Maugham)

Thus to say, to get the best in life you have to refuse the rest. Life does not give you what you deserve rather life gives you what you demand.

You must pay attention to things that you like doing. Those things you do and you don't want to stop doing are pointers to passion. As we have seen in the story of Manny Pacquiao, your passion is usually evident from early years of life. Other people too can see your tendencies and accurately determine what your passion is.

The failure to discover passion in most cases is due to the clouding of our minds by a number of factors. These mind clouding factors can be; other people's opinions of us, most especially those people who are close to us like parents, siblings, teachers or even pastors. Another clouding factor is the heroes we celebrate. Usually, these are people we want to be like for instance our role models and mentors. In trying to pick after their heroes, many people have lost sight of their own passion. Another factor is what you think of yourself. Remember, you are what you think. ***"For as he thinks within himself, so he is"***. You are defeated because you believe so.

All men come loaded into this earth with potential for greatness. Therefore the journey of discovery of passion and life calling should not be an impossible endeavor because passion is within you. I love what Oprah Winfrey said,

> *"Forget about the fast lane. If you really want to fly, harness your power to your passion. Honor your calling. Everybody has one. Trust your heart, and success will come to you".*

You are not buying passion with money but through careful self-inventory, you can discover the passion intrinsic to you. Few questions can assist you to discover and document your passion:

1. **What is the one thing I love doing?**

In most cases, a lot of people love doing more than one thing, but there is a need to settle on one prime focus. You don't have all the time in the world to try out everything you like. An attempt to do so will only end up in a wasted life. Settle on one passion that could be seconded by a few other things that you love.

2. **What one thing can I do with pleasure even without being paid?**

It is obvious that many people would dump any work that offers them no salary or monetary rewards because that is the only thing they gain from doing work. But if you gain more than just monetary rewards then you will cease to be under the base desire of survival. If we remove salary from your work would you still continue to do it?

3. **What observable things do I do best with ease?**

Other people can mislead you away from your passion but they can also guide you to your passion. Other people can point you to your passion. What is it that people know you for? Mostly in groups or teams, you will discover that people will give you tasks that they know you can do best with ease. You can depend on the observation of other people most especially those who are close to you like family.

4. **If there was only one thing I could do in life what would it be?**

When you have and engage in too many alternatives in life, you deplete much energy. Your passion requires maximum energy. If you were asked to do one thing for the rest of your life what one thing would it be? To discover "passion" you must focus on identifying that one thing.

When the name Manny Pacquiao crosses your mind, you think of boxing. When you talk about the game of golf, the name Tiger Woods rings a bell. You mention computer software the name Bill Gates crosses your mind. There is one passion that defines a person's life. What is your life's defining passion?

## DISCOVER TO RECOVER

Usually, people do tend to grow up into what their parents and society conditioned them to become. You must understand that the key to your success in this world is to discover the field of your calling. Also, realize that your gift is not what you do but who you are. Therefore to discover your passion is to discover yourself. Passion discovery is a critical component in your strategy to recover from society labeling.

The question to ask yourself is this, if you stop working for Uncle Sam, what happens next? You have to now turn your focus on to the things that you are passionate about.

When you discover your passion, you set yourself on a journey to a life of fulfillment and purpose. Engaging in the work of your passion entails recovery of true self. You are never truly yourself when you are not living your passion. You could be making good money but it will not do you any good in relation to self-actualization. Samuel Smiles says, *"He who never made a mistake, never made a discovery"*. That is to say, to make discoveries you have got to suspend the fear of making mistakes and go after your dream with maximum focus and energy.

We can learn from what Thomas Edison said, *"I have not failed. I've just found 10,000 ways that don't work"*. We should not relent till we discover our promised land. Of course, you don't need to make 10,000 attempts for you to discover your purpose. I encourage you to get my book titled **"Who am I, why am I here?"**. You must have this book in your library. And let me just say this, discovering your identity is the key to fulfilling your destiny. Therefore discover yourself and you would have made an important step towards your freedom from Uncle Sam.

## DEVELOPING YOUR PASSION

Passion development is personal development. I want you to think of personal development as *"a development which depends on inner reasons, regardless of external factors"*. Personal development entails self-analysis so as to live life to the fullest as opposed to waiting for things to happen by themselves.

What is worse than untapped talent is undeveloped talent. The journey does and should not end in passion discovery; there must be a deliberate growth initiative. There is a need to grow the work you are passionate about. Grow your talents, gifts, competencies to the highest level possible. This is the process of value creation.

Your gift, no matter how unique if not developed it will yield very little. There are many people who have succeeded not because of outstanding talent but because of outstanding dedication to the development of talent.

Development is always never easy but through hard work, it becomes the distinguishing factor. It requires discipline and hard work to develop your gift and talents. There are many people out there doing the same thing you are doing, offering the same services you are offering but if you develop what you have, it will attract people by itself.

When you stop growing you start dying. Life is all about growth; if your gifts and talents are not growing they are dying. You should always be growing, always developing, like the Chinese proverb says, ***"Be not afraid of growing slowly, be afraid only of standing still"***

It is your responsibility to ensure the growth of your passion. It is you who understands how you love doing what you do, so take personal responsibility for its development.

# WHAT YOU DON'T DEVELOP YOU LOOSE

"And unto one he gave five talents, to another two, and to another one; to every man according to his several ability; and straightway took his journey. Then he that had received the five talents went and traded with the same, and made them other five talents. And likewise he that had received two, he also gained other two. But he that had received one went and digged in the earth, and hid his lord's money. After a long time the lord of those servants cometh, and reckoneth with them. And so he that had received five talents came and brought other five talents, saying, Lord, thou deliv-eredst unto me five talents: behold, I have gained beside them five talents more.

His lord said unto him, Well done, thou good and faithful servant: thou hast been faithful over a few things, I will make thee ruler over many things: enter thou into the joy of thy lord. He also that had received two talents came and said, Lord, thou deliveredst unto me two talents: behold, I have gained two other talents beside them. His lord said unto him, Well done, good and faithful servant; thou hast been faithful over a few things, I will make thee ruler over many things: enter thou into the joy of thy lord.

Then he which had received the one talent

came and said, Lord, I knew thee that thou art an hard man, reaping where thou hast not sown, and gathering where thou hast not strawed: And I was afraid, and went and hid thy talent in the earth: lo, there thou hast that is thine. His lord answered and said unto him, Thou wicked and slothful servant, thou knewest that I reap where I sowed not, and gather where I have not strawed: Thououghtestthereforetohaveputmymoney to the exchangers, and then at my coming, I should have received my own with usury. Take therefore the talent from him, and give it unto him which hath ten talents. (emphasis mine) For unto every one that hath shall be given, and he shall have abundance: but from him that hath not shall be taken away even that which he hath. If you don't grow what you have you will lose it"

*Matthew 25:15 – 29*

This passage of scripture reveals some vital truths to us concerning putting our talents to profitable use.

1. All men have received gifts and talents; abilities with which they can engage in business (work) for profitability.

The scripture shows us that each servant received a talent with which he could engage in profitable trade. No man can excuse his lack of pursuing his God-given purpose because all men were created for a purpose; our duty is to discover and develop the talents and gift that enable us to fulfill our purpose. You have no need of competing with others; you have your own race to run. You have a special unique gift, talent, ability that you need to use as a means of doing work.

2. God is not expecting from us what we cannot deliver; He has gifted us according to what we are able to perform.

We also see in the scripture that when the master returned, he asked the servants to account for the talents he had left with each of them. Sometimes people get this sense of inadequacy when the theme of pursuing their God-given passion is brought to them. Everyone has within themselves what it takes to achieve the purpose God has called them to. God has equipped you for your calling, so be bold and go after it. God is expecting an account from you on the performance of the gifts and talents He gave you not on what you don't possess.

3. Different in quantity but not in importance, the master gave talents according to the ability of each servant

Whether president, medical doctor, engineer, teacher, cook or driver, all men have special gifts and talents from God. Dr. Martin Luther King Jr. expressed it this way, *"if a man is called to be a street sweeper, he should sweep streets even as Michelangelo painted, or Beethoven composed music or Shakespeare wrote poetry. He should sweep streets so well that all the hosts of heaven and earth will pause to say, here lived a great street sweeper who did his job well".* Your calling is as important as anybody else's. And God will require an account.

4. Growing (developing) what you have been given brings glory to God.

We can observe in the above scripture that the master was pleased with the two servants who multiplied the talents they received. The point here is that our master is pleased only when we present to him the profits of our endeavors. If you are working, fulfilling your purpose, you too can look forward to hearing the Lord say, "well done" if you develop your divine endowments.

5. You lose what you don't develop.

The scripture further tells us how the servant that buried the talent was castigated and condemned by his master for lack of enterprising initiative. It is laziness to neglect the gift and talents that God has given us. If you chose to sit idle and not put to work God's resources in you, He will entrust someone else and you will stand to lose. The wicked servant thought his master was losing by his laziness and neglect but he later discovered he was the one losing. God will not take laziness lightly; you've got to be busy growing your gifts and talents.

6. God judges our faithfulness by how we grow what he has given us.

Lastly, we can observe that the two servants who went to engage profitably with the master's talent were commended as being faithful. Faithfulness in God's economy is not you bringing back to him exactly what he originally gave to you. Faithfulness is multiplying or growing what you received. Returning more than you receive is faithfulness. Therefore faithfulness is profitable engagement in various enterprises by using the endowments we are born with. God counts you faithful if you put to profitable use all the resources he has put in you.

## START YOUR DAY
## THE JOBS WAY

*"I have looked in the mirror every morning and asked myself: "if today were the last day of my life, would I want to do what am about to do today?" And whenever the answer has been "No" for too many days in a row, I know I need to change something".*
(Steve Jobs)

If today was the last day of your life, would you want to do what you are about to do today? A '**yes**' to that questions means you are happy and passionate about your work. A '**no**' simply means you either have not discovered your passion or you are not taking steps to make changes about engaging in your passion.

The only work a person would love to do on the last day of his life would ultimately define his life passion. Mr. Jobs' every morning question will help to maintain focus on your passion as you journey on in life.

When you are about to go to work, ask yourself if really that is the last job you would love to do. Steve Job's every morning question will always keep you in check regarding your life calling and passion. This question will help you identify and curtail the things that keep you busy and occupied about matters that don't relate to your passion.

Just because you are busy does not always mean you are fulfilling your calling. You can be busy but busy at doing the wrong work. Never lose track of your passion; start your day the Steve Job's way.

In your quest to stop working for Uncle Sam it is paramount that you discover your passion and go on to do whatever it takes to grow it. I have already elaborated early that you need to make your passion you work. Make what you love doing become your work. It will take hard work and discipline to develop the work of your passion. If you grow and develop your gifts and talents you will be judged faithful in God's economy. Don't postpone any work you have to do in respect to discovering and developing your passion.

> *"Almost everything all external expectations, all pride, all fear of embarrassment or failure these things just fall away in the face of death, leaving only what is truly important. Remembering that you are going to die is the best way I know to avoid the trap of thinking you have something to lose. You are already naked. There is no reason not to follow your heart."*
> (Steve Jobs)

# CHAPTER 12
# GOLDEN POINTS

1. The discovery of that calling for your life is what sets you on a journey to your freedom from the bondage of Uncle Sam.

2. Discovery of passion will set you on the right career path thus your need for effort in discovering it.

3. The things you do and you don't want to stop doing are pointers to passion.

4. The journey to discover passion should not be an impossible endeavor because passion is within you.

5. When you have and engage in too many alternatives in life you deplete much energy.

6. When you discover your passion you set yourself on a journey to a life of fulfillment and purpose.

7. What is worse than untapped talent is undeveloped talent.

8. Grow your talents, gifts, competencies to the highest level possible.

9. Your gift, no matter how unique if not developed it will yield very little.

10. Development is always never easy but through hard work, it becomes the distinguishing factor.

11. When you stop growing you start dying. Life is all about growth

12. "If today were the last day of your life, would you want to do what you are about to do today?"

CHAPTER THIRTEEN

# ADD VALUE TO YOURSELF AND BEGIN TO OFFER YOUR SERVICES

*"Try not to become a man of success but try to become a man of value"*
*(Albert Einstein)*

In this chapter, we turn our focus to the aspect of value addition. From the onset I want you to understand that people won't pay you because you possess a gift, talent, passion or calling. Rather people will pay you for the benefit they get from it.

This is why not every movie maker is highly sought after. This is also the reason why not every book makes the bestseller list. The net worth of your gift or talent is proportional to its market value. Value, therefore, is "the degree of usefulness, importance or benefit of something".

A European missionary went to serve in a remote village of central Africa as a medical volunteer.

The area he was stationed was a literal gemstone mine. Every morning the villagers would gather precious stones on the banks of the river. They would decorate themselves with these stones around their necks and arms as ordinary ornaments.

The missionary seeing their ignorance offered to give

food items and money to anyone who brought him the best of the stones collected from the river.

Occasionally the missionary would travel to the capital city and take the stones brought to him for cutting and polishing. He would then consign his precious stones to his home country for a fortune.

One evening the villagers observed from a distance a glowing light from a hole they had been digging for a well.

In the morning they rushed to the hole and there at the base lay a beautiful stone.

The villager on whose farm the stone was discovered knew exactly what he would do with the stone. He saddled his bicycle and dashed to the missionary's tent. He showed the piece of stone to the missionary and demanded his reward.

After careful examination of the stone, the missionary knew that that was all he needed to live in luxury until death. He had hit the Jackpot.

The Missionary gave in local currency an equivalent of $100 bill to the villager and told him to take charge of his tent till he returned.

That was the last the villagers ever saw or heard of the missionary.

The villagers like most people never realized the value of what they possessed. Just that one stone was enough to build them a village hospital, school and sink better boreholes.

Your gift is like a rough diamond that is worth very little if it remains uncut and unpolished.

A few hours in the hands of a gemstone cutter a rough stone assumes a new identity. You would even mistake it for another. That's exactly what value addition does to your gift and talent.

Your raw gift, talent or even an anointing is worth very little but when you add value to it, it transforms into a piece of commodity highly valued by other people.

When you discover your gift or talent and convert it into a precious commodity through value addition, the whole world will seek you out.

## GROW YOUR VALUE

You should never neglect the aspect of value addition. Take for example in a game of soccer. Each team usually carries 22 players. The best 11 of those 22 get to make the first choice team while others wait for some unfortunate injury, failure or underperformance of any of the first choice players.

All the 22 players have the same chance of featuring in the first choice team but not all make it. They all train together but others go beyond the normally scheduled training session to do more on their own. While others eat anything, anytime and anyhow, there are those who watch their diet closely so as to maintain the best form for each game.

With the same ball, certain players dribble with individual signature moves that make the fans go wild while others just kick it around. Those signature moves are not taught or developed in group practice but in solitude hours of self-disciplined personal training.

All men are born equal having equal opportunities in life but the net worth they create differentiates them. We all have the same chance at the game of life but only those who produce more value become highly demanded.

Apart from just adding value, there are various interpersonal skills that will make you a winner in the place of your vocation. There are various ways that you could employ to add value to yourself. Many people have had great failures in attempting to set themselves free from Uncle Sam without sufficient preparation both in personality and investment money.

In your quest for freedom, knowledge is like a magnet for attracting money and wealth.

Anybody who has conquered Uncle Sam system to become wealthy and command money first had to know the "how" by which money operates. You too should study the laws of money while maintaining a balance on your attitude and mindset with God's word. Anywhere ignorance exists; there is an open door to a difficult life thus you cannot afford to remain or be in ignorance about any area pertaining to your life calling. So what can you do to enhance value addition to yourself?

## 1. "NANOS GIGANTUM HUMERIS INSIDENTES" – STAND ON SHOULDERS OF GIANTS

In every field of endeavor, there have been people that have gone ahead of you. "Nanos gigantum humeris insidentes" is an expression that illustrates the meaning of discovering truth by building on previous discoveries.

You will do well to learn from the giants of your discovered vocation. You may not see far by tip-toeing but by standing on shoulders of giants you will be able to see and accomplish great things beyond those who held you up. Let what other people have done and accomplished be your springboard to launch you into your greatness. You need to do everything possible to glean from the libraries of great men.

Look at people that have gained freedom from Uncle Sam and are doing what you desire to do. Emulate them and let their failures be your warnings and let their successes be your leverage.

> *"If I have seen further, it is by standing on the shoulders of giants"*
> (Isaac Newton)

There are giants that are no longer alive but their works still live on. It is your responsibility to get materials, tapes, books, articles etc. whatever you can get your hands on, that would enable you to interact with great minds of centuries past. Make a deliberate reading plan weekly, monthly and yearly.

You grow your capacity as you read more of what other people before you have written; capacity to handle what they could not handle. You will gain further wisdom to navigate the maze of life from their experiences.

If you resolve to change your thinking, you will surely change your attitude and ultimately your whole life.

When media mogul Tyler Perry's screenplay, I Know I've Been Changed became a sleeper hit that offered audiences a refreshing glimpse into the hard, and often times funny things, that God can deliver you from. He didn't end there. Perry stood on the shoulders of Bishop. T.D. Jakes. Taking Bishop Jakes' bestselling book 'Woman Thou Art Loosed' Tyler turned it into a stage production, a project that exploded into a blockbuster hit. He simply saw a giant that he could stand on for him to see further.

God would be wasting time to start revealing to you

what he has already revealed to other people. Be humble and read the works of other people.

> **"In the first year of his reign I Daniel understood by books the number of the years, whereof the word of the LORD came to Jeremiah the prophet, that he would accomplish seventy years in the desolations of Jerusalem. And I set my face unto the Lord God, to seek by prayer and supplications, with fasting, and sackcloth, and ashes".**
>
> *Daniel 9:2 – 3*

We can observe in this passage of scripture several things that are helpful for use in our quest to build on other people's revelations.

The scripture clearly shows us that Daniel understood by reading the writings of Jeremiah. He did not get a revelation from an angel, or by an audible voice. Daniel understood God's plan for his people by reading books of another man. Thus to say, that the more we read, the more we increase our capacity to be solution providers.

The passage also shows us yet another important aspect. We see that Daniel's prayer was a product of understanding. He didn't just rush to pray anyhow. He first sought understanding regarding the captivity his countrymen were suffering.

Today there are many Christians who rush to the mountain tops before they gain understanding thus their prayers are misdirected and consequently receive no answers.

You can also see in the scripture that Daniel was a prophet of God just like Jeremiah. Yet God didn't reveal to Daniel what he had already revealed to Jeremiah some 70 years before. The point here is that even if you are in the same field of calling with another person, it does not guarantee access to the same amount of knowledge. Therefore you must learn from other people.

For example; a pastor seeking church growth should not just rush to the mountain to get a revelation or unique growth strategy. You realize that in the same city or country, there are pastors who have managed to grow churches. Therefore the pastor seeking church growth should and must learn from his fellows.

## 2. MENTAL TRANSFORMATION THROUGH RIGOROUS STUDY

The mind is central to all change. If you can change your mind, you can change your life. The mind is vital in your journey of value addition.

> *"If you think you are beaten, you are. If you think you dare not, you don't. If you'd like to win, but think you can't it's almost a cinch you won't. Life's battles don't always go to the stronger or faster man, but sooner or later the man who wins is the one who thinks he can"*

You've got to let you mind revolve with the assignment of God for your life.

Think about how you could bring glory to God through your work. Feed yourself with God's word as regards your priority of serving him. Mental states affect our whole being and as such you must strive to renew your mind continually. By doing multiple readings of books like this one, your mind begins to be programmed accordingly thus setting you up for a successful and purpose fulfilling life.

**"For as he thinketh in his heart, so is he"**

*Proverbs 23:7.*

To transform your life you first have to transform your mind. Mental transformation will always lead to life transformation.

You can never go where your mind has never been. You cannot accomplish with your hands what you have not accomplished in your mind. Your hands cannot hold what your mind has not imagined.

If you don't make effort to study financial matters or even go for seminars, it is a sure sign of laziness – mental laziness. It doesn't matter how you labor physically but if your labors are not informed by a mental ascent and knowledge base then you are exhibiting laziness. As you desire to work for God and live independent of any system of bondage, strive to overcome all forms of mental laziness. Mental laziness is what sponsors many people in continuing to operate under Uncle Sam's bondage. May your story be different, aspire to life transformation through mental transformation.

## 3. GREAT COMPANY MAKES ONE GREAT

You must understand that it's either people are adding value to you or they are wasting your time (**LIFE**).

Through books, we enjoy the companies of those who have passed on. If we keep the company of great men, in reading their books, the value we obtain will be vivid for all to behold.

Great company makes one great. Likewise, insubstantial company makes one insubstantial. Care must be taken with regards to whom you allow to speak into your life.

Some of the giants whose company we need and must appreciate are still alive and approachable.

You have to make every effort to sign up for their seminars, mentorship programs etc. if possible getting to sit under their sanatorium. Take steps to discover who are those people, who hold the knowledge you need to make you a winner in the place of your calling.

The story of Kenneth Copeland is nothing short of remarkable in illustrating this concept. Almost unbelievable to many today, Kenneth Copeland lived in abject poverty until information brought transformation in his life. The story is that the desire for change in his life gave birth to a knowledge hunt.

Kenneth Copeland was driven to Kenneth Hagin's office in search of Hagin's message tapes and materials.

He was so desperate for insight that he wanted to trade off his car for the tapes. To his amazement, Hagin gave him the tapes free and he went on to lock himself up in a room and began to feed on heavenly information.

Through that knowledge, Kenneth Copeland has built a successful world-wide ministry commanding great wealth. Copeland's encounter with Hagin changed his life. You too must find the Hagin of your life.

## 4. CONSTANTLY APPLY THE LAW OF CONVERSION

To be a person who is adding value to your life, you

have to convert every moment into a measurable value increase to your life. You should, by all means, ensure that you organize your life in such a way that every activity you engage in is producing some sort of value for yourself or other people.

Every minute must be converted to added value. This can be achieved for example by listening to tapes on your way to the office or spending time with friends that are adding value to your life by challenging you to be better than you already are.

Carefully analyze areas of your life where you need more value. Then structure your daily activities in such a way as to ensure maximum benefit on your part. Everything you are doing must be contributing some value to your life.

## 5. DISCIPLINE AND HARD WORK

*"The price of success is hard work, dedication to the job at hand, and the determination that whether we win or loose, we have applied the best of ourselves to the task at Hand"*
*(Vince Lombardi)*

To grow your value you must become a workaholic. You must be a person who loves to work and to work hard. If you want to stop working for Uncle Sam you must begin to work hard and long. Do you know that successful people spend about 14 to 18 hours working? Success does not come cheaply. You've got to pay the price it takes.

It's not surprising that Lionel Messi is rated as soccer's most expensive player. He is estimated to be worth about $270 million.

His kind of success does not come on a silver platter. It is through hard work.

At only age 25, Messi has achieved what an average man cannot achieve in his lifetime. Being the most expensive footballer, many prestigious awards like The Footballer of the Year, UEFA Best Player in Europe and many others have been added to his accomplishment list.

Reading about Messi, I learned that he employs a workout program that requires hard work. Messi's training routines combine a series of movement work-outs and plyometric exercises meant to develop enhanced movement and coordination of his feet. The program also helps him to build up core strength needed to make a world class player.

Talent alone didn't make Messi become one of the world's most famous football players. Discipline and dedication to a rigorous workout routine and strict diet plan have made his name to be synonymous with football.

We can observe Messi has learned an important factor of success, **"HARD WORK"** As Malcolm Gladwell says, *"Hard work is a prison sentence only if it does not have meaning."*

> *"Opportunities are usually disguised as hard work, so most people don't recognize them".*
> *(Ann Lander)*

The quote illustrates to us that those who don't work hard always lose opportunities.

Daniel Levitin a Neurologist writes: *"After numerous studies, we came to see the following rule: whatever field one chooses to achieve, the level of skill commen-*

*surate with the status of a world-class expert, it requires 10,000 hours of practice. No matter whom you take — composers, basketball players, writers, skaters, pianists, chess players and inveterate criminals and soon we meet this figure with a surprising regularity. Ten thousand hours means approximately three hours of practice per day or twenty hours per week for the past ten years. Yet there is not a single case of a person who achieved the highest level of skill in a less period of time".*

Thus 10,000 practice hours in your field of endeavor will make you the best. Invest time in your passion through hard work, determination and discipline. And the kind of practice should be perfect practice like Vince Lombardi says,

> *"Practice does not make perfect, perfect practice makes perfect".*

## BE ON HIGH DEMAND

> *"One machine can do the work of fifty ordinary men. No machine can do the work of one extraordinary man*
> *(Elbert Hubbard)*

You can become extraordinary by adding value to yourself. You will be irreplaceable in your chosen field of work. Machines are slowly taking over the workplace. For example, the office of a few years ago had a typewriter demanding a typist. It had voluminous storage cabinets which have since been replaced by storage mediums like disks and memory sticks. The office place has evolved from hardware to software. Typists thought that they were irreplaceable. The computer proved superior. To stay relevant on the market you've got to constantly add value to yourself. Become superior.

People will pass you by if you offer inferior products and services. If you are not in demand it means you have not been efficient with the resources in your life.

As Zig Ziglar puts it, "*you can have everything in life you want if you'll just help enough people get what they want*" if your product or service is helping people get what they want, they will, in turn, pay you and you will be able to get what you want in life. The more people you help the more net worth you create for yourself.

You will grow the demand for your goods and service if you can meet the needs of more people. Offer more to more.

If you perfect your gift you will be in demand. If you are ill prepared you will fail to attract more people to engage with your calling, passion or business. The more skills you acquire the more you increase your ability to provide more solutions.

This is why it is important to gain all the relevant experience as you temporarily work for Uncle Sam. When you stop working for the system you would have equipped yourself to a level where you are the most sought after in your field.

Say for example your passion is music. If you then decide to just sit and watch TV all day long and eat anyhow instead of concentrating on adding value to your gift. If you don't discipline yourself to develop your vocal abilities and skills in playing some instrument, it's obvious that no one will care to listen to your music or buy your tapes.

While others are being offered recording deals by big labels, you will be running from agent to agent seeking connections.

With poor skill levels, you can forget about being in demand in Uncle Sam system for starters. And you definitely won't be able to do much working for yourself. Here is what you can do to be or remain in demand

## SHARPEN AND PACKAGE YOUR PASSION INTO A GREAT PERSONALITY

We are all a product of the people who brought us up, the environment we grew up in and later the choices we've made. You can remodel yourself to become the person of your dreams.

To be and remain in demand you must implement a dual development plan in your passion and skills.

**"If the iron be blunt, and he do not whet the edge, then must he put to more strength: but wisdom is profitable to direct"**

*Ecclesiastes 10:10*

Your passion is the iron but skill and personality development is the sharpening of that iron. If your passion is not sharpened you will struggle at even the simplest of jobs.

Without it you will not engage competitively in the labor market. You need the wisdom; that is, the '**knowhow**' of doing something. Wisdom in this regard means you have become a quality professional and you can manage to leave Uncle Sam system anytime to start your own work.

When your passion and calling corresponds to your skills then it does not matter even if you are working in Uncle Sam system because you will be able to bring the kingdom of God there without being compromised by the need for salary to survive.

Once your skills correspond with your calling invariably you will come to a level whereby even if you are working for somebody else it will be by your own terms. You will be so good at what you do that you can dictate the terms.

You will lack the power to bargain for good deals if your passion and skills are not developed to the highest possible level of proficiency.

Allow me to tell a story of the legendary Bruce Lee who lived and worked in the area of his passion.

Bruce moved to Seattle to live in an apartment over a Chinese restaurant owned by Ruby Chow, a friend of Bruce's father. Without inferiority, Bruce worked as a waiter downstairs to earn his keep.

At his coming back to San Francisco Bruce Lee only had $100 in his pocket, he had to work odd jobs in Chinese communities to survive.

Desiring to upgrade himself he enrolled in Edison Technical School to complete his high school diploma. It was at this time Bruce started teaching Chinese Kung Fu in parks and people's backyards.

This income combined with his earnings from his work in Ruby's restaurant, allowed him to enroll in the University of Washington in Seattle. Bruce Lee has been hailed by a multitude of people throughout the world in numerous ways as one of the most inspirational and formative figures in human history.

At the time when martial arts was secretive and exclusive to the Chinese and other eastern nations, Bruce Lee started a revolution in the west that embraced teaching anyone who wanted to learn no matter what their race, or ethnic background, experience, etc. White, Black, Asian whatever! His schools were highly patronized by a lot of people because he was not only teaching martial arts. His training came packaged in respect for humanity and celebration of life regardless of color and ethnicity.

As a result, after a short time of teaching non-Chinese students in Oakland, Bruce was challenged by a rival and leading Shaolin Kung Fu master from across the bay in San Francisco's Chinatown, named Wong Jack Man. The rivals saw Master Lee as a traitor and sought to restrain him. We see that competition can get escalated when you seem to thrive above your fellows.

Thus Bruce had accumulated enemies that bitterly hated him for *"betraying his people."* They saw him as a traitor. This, however, turned out to be a revolutionary and enormous leap forward for the strong willed Bruce, for the martial arts and for those who wanted freedom from hatred, racism, and prejudice.

Bruce Lee's talent for martial arts was developed by vigorous training under various masters including the renowned Wing Chun Master known as Yip Man.

His studies in philosophy helped Bruce to think differently thus developing a unique personal philosophy which led to the birth of his own system of fighting call Jeet Kune Do, Through a combination of Talent, education and constant personal development. He died a legend at age 33.

An important lesson in this story is that when your passion and calling corresponds to your skills then it does not matter even if you are working in Uncle Sam system you will be in charge of your life.

Bruce's rivals created a system that made success almost impossible for him. The system was "**THE**" big brother of the San Francisco martial arts world. You see Bruce either had to abandon his passion or engage in it at their dictates. Bruce defied the odds and publicly stated that he was able to defeat any martial artist in San Francisco. To make such a bold challenge one needed to be sure of himself. Wong Jack Man took him up on this. According to the challenge laid at Bruce's feet; if Bruce were to lose the challenge, he was either to close his school or put an end to his teaching of non-Chinese people.

Linda, Lee Bruce's wife recounts the encounter, she says "within minutes" Wong's men were trying to stop the fight, as he was ignominiously running from Bruce. The farce ended as Bruce dragged his challenger to the ground and pounded him into submission". When you are good at what you do you will never bow down to the system.

You've got to develop your gift or talent so that it becomes a money-making enterprise. Thereafter you must package it in a salable personality.

And as you help more people get value from your gift or talent, you too will be getting your God given freedom of working to express your true self.

# CREATE PRODUCTS AND SERVICES

As already discussed in an early chapter, Life, in economic terms defines two groups of people. There are those who buy goods and services. And secondly, there are people who create and sell goods and services. I am sure you remember the Esaus and Jacobs. The question is; to which group or category of people do you belong?

If you are working for Uncle Sam it is obvious that you are in the group of people who buy goods and services (consumers). You might be part of the system that creates and sell goods but not for your benefit. You are just a piece of the production process; no much different from the machinery of a manufacturing production line. In this case, Uncle Sam is the one who usually creates and sells goods and services.

If you desire to stop working for Uncle Sam you must think more in terms of production rather than consumption. Work hard at converting your God given gift and talent into a tangible, salable product or service.

> *"Happiness lies in the joy of achievement and the thrill of creative effort".*
> *(Frank-lin D. Roosevelt)*

If you are going to be free from Uncle Sam system you need to be creative. You've got to think of ways of making life better for other people and they will definitely come for your offers.

You will be producing goods and service not for Uncle Sam's profitability but for your own financial liberty so that you can glorify God in obeying Him to the latter.

When considering how to stop working for Uncle Sam, it is prudent for people to know that they leave Uncle Sam to go and work profitably in their land of purpose and not to sit and wait for miracles. Just sitting in church and waiting for a miracle is not being creative, that's being lazy.

## OFFER YOUR PRODUCTS AND SERVICES

Most talented people like writers, scientist and the likes, lock themselves in laboratories with great products which never reach the buying public. People have written books that have just ended up as good ideas, never being published. People need to know what you are offering. Look for what products and service people are craving for that relate to your passion and innovate products and service that will satisfy the demand or deliver the required solutions.

> *"You can't advertise today and quit tomorrow. You're not talking to a mass meeting. You're talking to a parade."*
> *(Bruce Barton, 1930)*

The scaling of any mountain requires persistence. You can't just produce goods and service and sit down reflecting upon what a great product you have created. You've got to go out there and convince the people to buy your product.

You don't have to be sophisticated but simply educate the buying public about your product. And with the right niche you will be able to grow into your life's calling.

With a worldwide audience through social media on

platforms like Facebook, YouTube and many more platforms you can reach millions. Your potential buyers in this digital, electronic world are simply a click away.

> *"To live a creative life we must lose the fear of being wrong"*
> *(Joseph Chilton Pearce)*

# CHAPTER 13
# GOLDEN POINTS

1. Anywhere ignorance exists; there is an open door to a difficult life

2. Mental transformation will always lead to life transformation.

3. Great company makes one great, likewise insubstantial company makes one insubstantial.

4. The more skills you acquire the more you increase your ability to provide more solutions.

5. If you don't make effort to study financial matters or even go for financial consultation is a sure sign of laziness – mental laziness.

6. When your passion and calling corresponds to your skills then it does not matter even if you are working in Uncle Sam system because you will be able to bring the kingdom of God there without being compromised by the need for salary to survive.

## CHAPTER FOURTEEN

# BUILD STRATEGIES FOR KINGDOM LIVING

A strategy is defined as a plan designed to achieve a particular long-term aim. Remember in this section am giving you strategies of how to stop working for Uncle Sam. Apart from getting your priorities right, discovering and developing your passion, adding value to yourself and offering your products and service you've got to have a kingdom strategy.

You must develop a clear course of action that shows how you will be manifesting the Kingdom of God.

Your plan must take into account the specifications of resources required to achieve a specific goal. Will you need money? How many people will you influence? What results are you expecting to see? As you ask yourself these questions you will begin to get a clear plan for kingdom impact.

We have seen so far how that the purpose of work in God's economy is not for survival but for kingdom growth. Thus as we work for Uncle Sam, we should include in your plan a strategy of propagating the Kingdom of God.

The motive for desiring freedom from the system is not so that we can have personal income to meet our daily needs. By now you know that our needs are met through God's providence when His Kingdom becomes central in our lives. When you devote yourself to the promotion of God's kingdom you can prepare yourself for blessings.

You should desire to be free so that you can do what you were originally created to do, thereby glorifying your creator.

Building strategies for the advancement of God's kingdom should take center stage as we plan to stop working for Uncle Sam.

This may seem to be a very tasking undertaking but that's what we are called to do; to influence society with kingdom values and principals. We should desire to see heaven being replicated on the earth. If God requires this of you, it's because he has equipped you in advance.

## A CALL WITHIN A CALL

On 10th September 1946, Agness Gonxha Bojaxhiu popular known as Mother Teresa received what she called *"a call within a call"*. She expressed this call through her mission statement, *"to quench the infinite thirst of Jesus on the cross for love and souls" by "laboring at the salvation and sanctification of the poorest of the poor"*. Mother Teresa did not ignore that call. She did not silence what she felt inside her heart to just find a job and earn a salary.

The implementation and operation of that call went on to give rise to Missionaries of Charity family of sisters, brothers, fathers and co-workers.

We see that Mother Teresa had to formulate a strategy which was recognized by the Indian prime Minister and the Roman Catholic. She was thereafter given necessary support. In 1952 she opened her first hospice. With the help of the Indian government, she was able to convert a Hindu temple into a home for the dying poor.

The strategy was to establish mission centers through

which her calling of reaching the poor people with Jesus' love was to be achieved. She would minister the love of Jesus, helping the poor while living among the poor. Her philosophy was that being unwanted, unloved, uncared for, forgotten by everybody, was much greater hunger, a much greater poverty than the person who has nothing to eat.

Mother Teresa once said, *"I am not sure exactly what heaven will be like, but I do know that when I die and it comes time for God to judge us, He will NOT ask us, How many good things have you done in life? Rather He will ask, how much LOVE did you put into what you did"*. Love was the theme of her work. You see that her love and concern for the stranded poor didn't just end in pity. She converted that love and concern into kingdom business that brought visible impact.

Her mission went beyond the borders of India on to be a worldwide phenomenon of mercy. In 1979 Mother Teresa was awarded the Nobel Peace Prize. Indira Gandhi once said, *"There are two kinds of people, those who do the work and those who take the credit. Try to be in the first group; there is less competition there"*. Those who knew her personally would testify that Mother Teresa belonged to that first group. God is faithful; in time her work was recognized and rewarded.

Dear reader your desire to be free from Uncle Sam should be motivated by a desire to become a kingdom propagator. As we see through one of Mother Teresa quotes, *"I am a little pencil in the hand of a writing God who is sending a love letter to the world"*. When you stop working for Uncle Sam, you invariably place yourself in the hands of God so that you can express his love in the sphere of your calling. You are God's love letter sent to the world of media, arts and entertainment, business, politics etc. don't conceal that letter in an envelope of Uncle Sam employment.

There is a call within you. Your abilities and passions all point to that calling. If you still have not gotten my book **"WHO AM I, WHY AM I HERE"**, you must get it. The book will help you to settle the question of your calling.

## WORK WITH ONLY ONE PURPOSE IN MIND

Like Mother Teresa, you should be concerned with *"quenching the infinite thirst of Jesus"*. In this case, yours is the expansion of the kingdom of God and His righteousness. Jesus changed our priority list; we are no longer living the Maslow's hierarchy of needs.

We are living according to the master's plan; his kingdom and righteousness are 'P1'. I have put forth this story of Mother Teresa to show you that the need for salary should no longer be driving you. Love for God and his kingdom must begin to consume you so much so that what defines your life is the pursuit of His kingdom. Christians should go to work with only one purpose in mind; to bring the kingdom of God in that sphere of life God has called them to.

We are called to conquer the world of medicine, politics, entertainment and education etc. for our God. To influence these spheres, we need a strategy.

Christians are supposed to saturate the various spheres of influence with God's principles and values.

You must realize that God transformed you so that you could transform your culture.

Christians should realize that salary is not the goal. The understanding we should have is that we work to manifest the kingdom of God. We should be constantly asking ourselves questions that will help us to maintain the kingdom focus. In order to help you develop your unique kingdom expansion strategy here are some questions for you to answer:

1.  What area of my work is dominated by evil that I can bring change to?

Because Christians have for a long time stood by and allowed the devil to dominate, morals have decayed drastically. There are things happening around your work environment that do not glorify God. You have been placed there to bring the required change.

The injustice that characterizes most institutions has never been changed because Christians who work there have focused on survival and not the kingdom of God. They are still in the bondage of Uncle Sam System.

The corruption that stamps the world of politics, for example, could be an evil that you recognize and plan to bring Godly principles to. Mother Teresa once said,

> *"Being unwanted, unloved, uncared for, forgotten by everybody, I think that is a much greater hunger, a much greater poverty than the person who has nothing to eat".*

She saw an evil that burdened her heart and she imagined what Jesus' response would be and responded in like manner.

Expressing the love of Jesus to the forsaken became her kingdom impact signature. What is your kingdom impact signature?

When the problem of AIDS reached to her heart, she responded as Jesus would. On Christmas Eve of 1985, she opened a home hospice for AIDS patients in New York. The point I am making here is that instead of com-plaining about the problems around you, decide to make a difference like Eleanor Roosevelt says, "Better to light a candle than curse the darkness".

That is being kingdom minded; looking for opportunities of expressing God's love and truth to the world. Every effort no matter how little makes a difference quoting Mother Teresa's words, she said: ***"Do not wait for leaders; do it alone, person to person"***. Don't wait to make a huge impact. The seemly small insignificant steps to kingdom expansion you make will echo in eternity as gargantuan leaps.

2. What can I do to reflect God's Light and righteousness?

After you identify the areas in your work environment that you can affect with Godly principles, you then need to realize something about who you are in Christ.

It is important to know that in Christ you have been given the authority to superimpose kingdom principles at your workplace.

You have been positioned on a mountaintop and your light must shine for all to see.

**"Ye are the light of the world. A city that is set on an hill cannot be hid. Neither do men**

**light a candle, and put it under a bushel, but on a candlestick; and it giveth light unto all that are in the house. Let your light so shine before men, that they may see your good works, and glorify your Father which is in heaven"**

*Matthew 5:14 – 16*

This passage informs us of our importance in this world. You are the light God has introduced in the dark. You are the light God has introduced in the world of politics, media, business, arts and entertainment etc. Don't hide your light because of the base desire for survival.

Your presence in your workplace should not permit evil because you are shining. You see, light shines in the darkness and the darkness cannot overcome it. Don't be afraid of the evil, rather the evil should be afraid of you. You can overcome all manner of darkness no matter how gross. This understanding will help you gain an attitude of boldness and courage to enforce change.

> *"People are like stainless glass windows, they sparkle and shine when the sun is out but when darkness sets in their true beauty is revealed only if there is a light from within".*
> *(Elizabeth Kubler-Ross)*

3. How can I affect my work environment with the principles and values of the kingdom of God?

One of the most important activities in human existence is asking questions and asking the right questions. The "**HOW**" question is cardinal as it defines the means or methods for achieving something. There is a lot you can do to impact your workplace with kingdom principles and values.

For example, you can introduce a lunch hour fellowship at your workplace; perhaps you could even start a business executive forum that meets to discuss various matters relating to the industry while being guided by Godly principals.

There are many ways to bring kingdom relevance. Perhaps you could think of introducing a *"mutual respect"* policy in your company and hold people accountable for the way they treat each other regardless of seniority. You could bring about a greater good by taking what may seem to be little steps of intervention.

> **"But ye shall not be so: but he that is greatest among you, let him be as the younger; and he that is chief, as he that doth serve"**
>
> *Luke 22:26*

Just this passage alone can be your top management philosophy. You can use it to inform top management attitude and practice thereby fostering the respect of human life. You could inculcate the principle of *"Servant – Leadership"* to overcome bully leadership attitudes. This is another example to illustrate to you that the ocean of possibilities is exhaustible. There are many ideas and strategy for you to influence your promised land.

Let me give you another idea of kingdom influence strategy from the above passage of scripture. You can initiate a top management day of service; where top management can engage in what may seem as insignificant and unimportant jobs like cleaning of surroundings. This would give the elite a higher appreciation of the lower ranking workforce. Just as there are many areas and fields of calling so are the ways in which you can bring the kingdom of God into manifestation.

When you are bent on establishing the kingdom of God in your workplace, strategies will come to your mind and grace is always given to implement and accomplish God's will.

God has called you to something great. It is beyond merely working for a salary. You are called to answer a particular problem for humanity.

If you remain in captivity of merely working for survival you won't realize what gift you've carried from eternity to bless humanity.

Therefore as you work towards freedom from Uncle Sam you need to develop kingdom strategies. These are ways and means of extending God's kingdom in the area of your influence. Become a kingdom minded person!

> *History calls those men the greatest who have ennobled themselves by working for the common good; experience acclaims as happiest the man who has made the greatest number of people happy.*
> *(Marx, Reflections of a Young Man (1835)*

# CHAPTER 14
# GOLDEN POINTS

1. Building strategies for the advancement of God's kingdom should take center stage as we plan to stop working for Uncle Sam.

2. We should desire to see heaven being replicated on the earth.

3. Jesus changed our priority list; we are no longer living the Maslow's hierarchy of needs. We are living according to the master's plan; his kingdom and righteousness are 'P1'.

4. Christians should go to work with only one purpose in mind; to bring the kingdom of God in that sphere of life God has called them to.

5. Your presence in your workplace should not permit evil because you are shining.

6. When you are bent on establishing the kingdom of God in your workplace, strategies will come to your mind and grace is always given to implement and accomplish God's will.

## CHAPTER FIFTEEN

# KNOW AND PERFECT THE LAWS OF MONEY

*"If you want to feel rich, just count all the things you have that money can't buy"*
*(Teasy)*

Being rich is more than just having cash in your pocket or bank account. Remember we are still discussing ways in which you could set yourself free from Uncle Sam system. This chapter is not enough to exhaust the material on knowing and perfecting the Laws of money, therefore, I would like to recommend that you get hold of my book; **"Money Won't Make You Rich"**. The book is a complete reading that will equip you with all the knowledge you need on the laws of money.

In this section, I seek to just elaborate to you that you can never be free from Uncle Sam system if you have not mastered and perfected the laws of money.

You will be operating against these laws if you don't know them. Laws have no respect for nationality, race, and sex or any other distinctive classification. Gravity is gravity, to Americans, Chinese, and Africans etc. Thus if you employ the laws that have made other people successful then you too will become successful. First of all, let me highlight to you some universal principles about "LAWS" relating to money matters.

## LAWS DON'T SEGREGATE

*"There are only two ways to live life.*
*One is as though nothing is a miracle.*
*The other is as if everything is".*
*(Albert Einstein)*

Most people are just waiting for miracles to happen but the reality is that this world was created to operate by laws and principles and not by miracles.

If you are going to stop working for Uncle Sam and begin working in the place of your calling, pleasing and glorifying God then you need to begin living your life by strict observance of laws of money.

No matter your status today, you can begin to apply the laws and you too will experience the change. As mentioned already, Laws have no respect for nationality, race, and gender or any other distinctive classification.

If you ignore universal laws, they will frustrate you. If you want to break them they will in turn break you. Laws are always constant and thus a life lived by laws and principles can be predicted. If you are applying the laws of money then I can predict with certainty that you will be free from Uncle Sam system sooner.

The cardinal point I am making here is that "**LAWS**" don't segregate. Women, just like men have the same opportunity to stop working for Uncle Sam by applying the Laws of money.

Knowledge and application of the laws of money will ensure that you transition smoothly to working for yourself or to having money work for you.

History will testify of America's first business superstar John D. Rockefeller and Andrew Carnegie the titan of the industrial age who made billions in the railroad and steel industries, who are celebrated among America's greatest philanthropists.

Will Smith dramatically retells the story of Chris Gardner in a movie *"The Pursuit of Happiness"*. Chris is pictured to come from a life of hardships but grew into success through hard work forming his own firm, Gardner Rich & Co which he later sold in a multimillion dollar deal.

The adopted Michael Oher, born in Memphis to a family of 12, Oher's mother was a crack cocaine addict and his father was in and out of prison is one of NFL accomplished players. The Body Builder governor Arnold Schwarzenegger, The rapper Shawn Corey Carter popularly known as Jay-Z, the queen of daytime TV Oprah Winfrey and many others.

All these stand to testify that in the world of money neither gender, ethnicity, college education or religious beliefs matter. Laws don't segregate. Christian or non-Christian, black or white, money comes to and increases in the hands of anyone who learns, understands, perfects and operates the laws of money.

## LET'S DESTROY SOME WRONG VIEWS

There are a lot of myths about money and how it operates. By wrong views I mean, those ideas, customs, or doctrines considered as being immune from criticism or question. Some of these wrong views have been with Christians for some time. People are afraid to bring them under scrutiny for the fear of an outcry from the masses.

But I want to dissipate several of the wrong views that modern Christendom has held dear. These wrong views are killing the church of Christ with regards to money matters. If you are going to stop working for Uncle Sam you need to discard these wrong views, and begin to educate yourself in the Laws of Money.

### Wrong view number One: Playing Lottery in Church to get Money

One of the principles of money is that it does not answer to religious gymnastics. If money was earned through spiritual exercises like prayer, fasting or tithing then only Christians would be wealthy.

The African Church has had a share of its own drama when it comes to money matters. People are seen carrying big carrier bags to church on Sundays announced as **"Miracle Money Sunday"**. The Pastor will give a prayer, commanding money to enter into the bags of the congregants. Then he will ask the congregants to open their bags and check for money. This culture is spreading like wildfire in most African countries and giving birth to an unhealthy greed for money among Christians.

I saw a Facebook post where one person posted saying, *"I prophesy to the first 400 fingers to type: Fire and share this post, miracle money enter your hand in Jesus Name"*. I thought to myself, "this is ridiculous", money does not come by typing Fire or sharing a Facebook post. Money comes by learning and operating the laws of money.

You see, instead of Christians being masters of money they are being cultured as slaves to money. Instead of engaging in producing goods and service for income, misled Christians are sitting in pews waiting for money to enter their bags. In most of these cases, the pastor will claim, "Angels of money are putting money in your accounts, bags, and pockets".

Christians are expecting miracles while non-Christians are on the move making money work for them through understanding and operating the laws of money. If you are going to stop working for Uncle Sam then you have to know how to stay and live free from Uncle Sam's bondage. When you stop working for Uncle Sam you don't go and sit in church believing God for miracle money. You need to engage in profitable enterprises.

In this era of miracle money Christians would rather spend hours in some religious cantata. They think that is the way they glorify God instead of engaging their hands in doing work that brings glory to God. You need to understand that money is not a miracle; it must either be earned or created.

When Christians just sit in church and don't make any attempt to create or earn money, they are no different from the gamblers playing the lottery in the casinos. We have seen how with the spread of Neo-prophetic movement African Christians would rather sit and just keep waiting for a miracle of some sort to bring them out of poverty instead of working. As you stop working for Uncle Sam the mindset you need to have is to firmly believe that you need to work to make money and then send that money out to work for you. When I say stop working for Uncle Sam I don't in a way infer that you stop work at all. Stop working for Uncle Sam is for the purpose of engaging in hard work in the field of your calling and purpose.

### Wrong view number Two: Money and wealth come to good people

Let me point it out clearly; you don't become wealthy because you are a good person. Otherwise, all the good people in the world would be wealthy. As a matter of fact in most societies, most of the wealthy people are not the good people. I have actually heard many people complain about why the bad people are the only ones that have all the money while the good people wallow in poverty. Some have even alleged that it is counterproductive to be good because then you will be poor. The truth, however, is that money doesn't come to either good or bad people. Money only comes to people who know the laws of money whether they are good or bad. Herein lays another universal principle of money. Money is neutral.

### Wrong view number Three: Money comes to those who do business

In most cases, people desiring wealth and financial prosperity believe that if they start their own business the story will change. The truth is that Money doesn't come to you because you do business. If that were true then all business people would be wealthy.

Everyone today is starting one sort of business with a view of gaining financial freedom. Most people today want to become or be called entrepreneurs. How many businessmen do you know around you? Are they all very rich? No! In most cases, people who do business, are not even aware of these laws of money.

Business is not the way out but a sound working knowledge of the Laws of Money. To me, it is indeed pathetic that many people who have been involved in business for a few decades cannot even boast of a million US dollars. This is primarily because they are laboring without the necessary knowledge of the vital laws of money. Kindly note the phrase "necessary knowledge", I'll elaborate on that in just a bit.

**WRONG VIEW NUMBER FOUR: YOU WILL BECOME RICH AND WEALTHY BECAUSE YOU ARE A CHRISTIAN**

Realistically speaking, you don't become rich because you are a Christian. Even though God promise wealth and prosperity, it is only on the condition that you abide by the laws of money.

> **"And you shall remember the LORD your God, for it is He who gives you power to get wealth, that He may establish His covenant which He swore to your fathers, as it is this day.**

*Deuteronomy 8:18*

In this passage, the Bible says God gives us the power to make wealth. Notice that God doesn't give wealth. He gives the power to get it. Unfortunately, in most cases, Christians are still hoping and thinking that just because they are Christians, God is obliged to give them wealth. No, sir, the correct understanding is that God gives you the skills that enable you to create wealth. God doesn't give wealth, but he gives you the power to go and get wealth. Potentially all Christians are wealthy but only those who operate the laws of money actualize their wealth.

Unfortunately, many prosperity gospel preachers have led the body of Christ astray by teaching that if Christians would only give, that that would bring prosperity to them. Regrettable to note that, some preachers even go to the extent of saying that the more you give, the more prosperous you will become. Allow me to emphatically state that giving alone won't make you rich. Experience and reality have proven that the doctrine ("of give and grow rich") is not totally true.

Sadly the over trusting and undiscerning masses have given and out given themselves, leading them to poverty and wretchedness rather than prosperity and abundance.

### "… and the wealth of the sinner is laid up for the just".

*Proverbs 13:22*

Other Christians sadly enough, are still waiting for when the wealth of the wicked will come to them. Yes, even though there is a scripture that talks about that, that scripture has been taken out of context. The wealth of the world will only come to you if you are good enough in what you do because the Israelites were good at what they did in Egypt before the wealth of Egypt came to them. As Vince Lombardi puts it, ***"The quality of a person's life is in direct proportion to their commitment to excellence, regardless of their chosen field of endeavor"***. The truth is that excellence in what Christians do and produce will lead to wealth transfer.

Secondly, the wealth of the world will only come to you if you produce better products than your competitors, that is when you are a good representative of the Kingdom of God and God will honor you for that.

Thirdly, for any wealth to come to you, you must be

busy producing either goods or rendering services. If you are only claiming promises, you will end up being disappointed at the end of the day.

For Christians to begin to enjoy the blessings of prosperity and wealth, it is high time churches began to teach and educate their members, not just on how to give and sow seeds, but also in how to produce goods and services. The reality is that there is no prosperity without production of goods or services.

### WRONG VIEW NUMBER FIVE: NAME IT, CLAIM IT AND HAVE IT!

Dear reader, money does not come to you because you name it and claim it. The "name it and claim it" philosophy has been popularized by what is known in Christendom as **"The Faith Movement"**. Most people just name and claim and then sit and wait for a manifestation. It is unfortunate that Christians spend hours, day in day out, naming and claiming but never having.

The Bible tells us in the book of Proverbs that *"In hard work, there is always profit, but too much chattering leads to poverty"*. After naming and claiming, you need to show diligence in your work. You need to show the virtue of hard work. You need to display your dedication to the principle of the dignity of labor. For money to truly come to you, you must go ahead to prove your obedience to some laws of money. Naming and claiming will not do it alone.

# GET TO KNOW THE WINNING WAYS

### WINNING WAY NUMBER ONE: "NECESSARY KNOWLEDGE" BRINGS WEALTH

*"Problems cannot be solved at the same level of awareness that created them"*
*(Albert Einstein)*

Here is another universal principle about money. Money favors those who master it through knowledge while punishing the ignorant. Expert knowledge in any field will make a man a winner. You are what you are today because of what you know or don't know. You are a sum total of your knowledge. Do you realize that you are in servitude today because of lack of knowledge? If you are to move from where you are today, you must start with gaining knowledge about where you are, where you want to be and what it takes to get there. The right knowledge is the key to success in any field of life. Knowledge of aerodynamics will make you a winner is the field of aerodynamics. But if you want to win in the field of real estate, the laws of aerodynamics will not give you success.

I want you to know that different sets of laws apply to different fields of life. The fact that you are a Professor, Doctor in Linguistics, Accounting or Mathematics does not guarantee you success in the field of money. You need to master the Laws of money if you are going to be a winner in the field of money. If you are going to be a winner in the field of money you need to acquire accurate knowledge. Money only comes to those who understand and master it.

One of the things that got my attention when I was doing a live broadcast on this topic was that many viewers hinted to how even with their University Degrees in Accounting and Finance, Business, and Account or other finance related fields never learnt what I was teaching. In most cases, many remarked having spent precious years and money but were never equipped with what it really takes to be free from Uncle Sam. Accurate knowledge is the key; go after it, as Benjamin Franklin says

> *"If a man empties his purse into his head, no man can take it away from him. An investment in knowledge always pays the best interest"*

Spend your money on the right knowledge. Gaining knowledge will cost you money and even when money is not available it will cost you the most important asset you have; your time.

**WINNING WAY NUMBER TWO: STOP LISTENING TO THE DICTATES OF MONEY**

What do you call that feeling you get when you've got some good cash in your pocket? I mean that confidence you get to enter any shop and ask for a price catalog of items you never budgeted for. Money talks and many people don't understand its language. Well, another thing you need to do is stop listening to the dictates of money. Money has a voice and it will constantly speak. When money enters your hands, the voice will either tell you to immediately spend it or save it for investment.

As is the case with most people, the voice of invest-ment is quickly put on mute and the voice (urge) to spend is amplified. To be a master over money you must stop listening to its dictates. You should disdain money to such an extent that it does not move your heart every time it flashes in your eyes. If money is your slave then you are on your way to stop working for Uncle Sam. It means that you have overcome the grip of money.

Don't allow money to control you rather be the one controlling money. Mastery over money entails; *"you sending out money to work for you and all you do is control (manage) it; commanding it to bring in the harvest"*.

### WINNING WAY NUMBER THREE: WORK TEMPORARY FOR UNCLE SAM TO RAISE CAPITAL

As already discussed, you must determine how many months or years it would take you to save up a deter-mined investment amount. Saving is important. I must remind you that working for Uncle Sam should not be to retirement as stipulated by the system but within 3 to 5 years could be enough for you to have saved up some startup capital.

> **"Then the steward said within himself, What shall I do? for my lord taketh away from me the stewardship: I cannot dig; to beg I am ashamed". "And the lord commended the unjust steward because he had done wisely: for the children of this world are in their generation wiser than the children of light"**
>
> *Luke 16:3,8*

Why did the Lord commend this unjust servant? The passage elaborates to us that the unjust servant realized three things: first that he was losing his work and secondly that he could not cultivate and thirdly he couldn't move around the city begging. We can observe that Jesus commended him because he used his position to buy social capital. He secured his future by using the very system that employed him. And Jesus said, "The children of this world are in their generation wiser than the children of light".

From this scripture, we can glean the several important facts about temporarily working for Uncle Sam. Let's look at these important facts for now:

### 1. Take a careful personality Inventory before you stop working for Uncle Sam

The scripture shows us that having heard the news of his impending dismissal, the steward was able to sit down and conduct an honest evaluation of himself. He recognized two important weakness in his life; firstly, he identified that he couldn't dig; that is being able to farm. Secondly, we see that he concluded that he was a shy person who could not go around begging. He looked at himself, honestly evaluating every aspect of his life. Likewise, it is important before you stop working for Uncle Sam that you conduct an honest self-evaluation. This will help you to know the pitfalls to avoid as you go to work for yourself in the place of your calling and purpose.

### 2. Make people who patronize your workplace indebted to you

Here is the second lesson we can learn from this passage. The character (the unjust servant) we considering could not work the farm late alone move around the city begging. He quickly came up with a plan. He needed to do something that would ensure people would be obliged to show him favor even without him begging for it. By giving favors to those who desperately needed it at his workplace the unjust servant secured favor for himself.

The point here is that how you do your work for Uncle Sam will either open or shut doors when you finally go to work for yourself. Make people you encountered in the course of daily duty be indebted to you. They will have no option but to also show the same favor.

3. **You should engage in work to raise both social and financial capital.**

The children of this world are wiser Jesus said because they perceive a rainy day and prepare for it. The steward in Jesus parable, based on personal inventory was able to determine his weaknesses and deficiencies. He built bridges that would ensure his survival after stopping work. You must build a social and financial bridge while you are still working for Uncle Sam. That is wisdom;

**"Go to the ant, thou sluggard; consider her ways, and be wise: Which having no guide, overseer, or ruler, Provideth her meat in the summer, and gathereth her food in the harvest"**

*Proverbs 6:6 – 8*

The ant has sharpened her sense of foresight that she is able to discern future seasons and she prepares herself. Without a guide, overseer or ruler ants can mobilize themselves and gather food to last for months. The ants have learned the art of being free from the dominion of any system.

### 4. Don't leave the system without anything

The last nugget we glean from the parable is that you should not take the step of stopping to work for Uncle Sam with empty hands. Your hands must have something that will help you to settle in the place and work of your passion. The emergency to stop working for Uncle Sam must not be done with your eyes closed. It is a step to be taken with well-calculated plans, strategies, and adjustments. Lack of preparedness is what sponsors failure in people who desired to stop working for the system. And in just a few months or years they had to return; looking for a job.

### WINNING WAY NUMBER FOUR: DON'T EAT YOUR SEED

> *"When you save your money, you're not depriving yourself of anything. You're actually buying yourself the most valuable thing you can: your freedom."*

From the outset, I want to emphatically state that when I say plant your seed I am not referring to the gimmicks of 'the prosperity gospel' which asks people to give money to some church program. That is manipulation meant to enrich a few individuals and not to give you the opportunity to stop working for Uncle Sam. The kind of investing (sowing seeds) I am talking about is investing in real tested methods of multiplying money and not some get rich quick formulas. I am not talking about positive confession or mental ascents that just bring people frustrations as they wait to harvest what they did not sow. The difference between the poor and the rich is that the poor man eats his seed while the rich invests it and later eats the overflows of the harvest.

When it comes to the prosperity message the teaching is that one prospers only when he gives thus, placing the emphasis on the wrong activity; giving only.

As I have already emphasized, if you want to be rich work for yourself, desire to learn and clearly understand the laws of money.

The temptation you will face the moment you stop working for Uncle Sam is the pressure to start spending from the raised capital on meeting needs. The capital you gain in the system is for investment and not to be used on any other thing. You may need to make downward adjustments in your lifestyle so you can be sustained through the period that your money is invested and growing.

You too can stop working for Uncle Sam but one thing is required, you must know and perfect the Laws of Money.

**"Wisdom is of utmost importance, therefore get wisdom, and with all your effort work to acquire understanding".**

*Proverbs 4:7 – ISV*

To conclude this chapter allow me to share my own personal story of how the Lord helped me with regards to money.

There was a point as a pastor I lived like everybody else. At that time our church was making 20,000 US dollars a month, surprisingly before the end of the month, we were already in the red. It was catastrophic until the Lord pointed out to me to read the story of the 3 servants and the talents. While reading the story, I kept on comforting myself that I was a good servant, because

I had a big church at that time and people were grateful to me for the changes and differences, that God had used me to make, in their lives.

What a shock it was to me when God told me that in this story I wasn't the good servant, I was not even the second servant that got two talents. What totally devastated me was when the Lord told me that I was worse than the last servant whom He condemned in that parable. My sense of pride and self-worth was so much offended that I was angry with God momentarily. I felt it was, by all means, unfair to have compared me to a wicked and lazy servant. But to now say I was worse than him totally shattered and ruined my day. I needed proof and an explanation. Then God began to take me to school.

He said, at least in the case of the wicked and lazy servant, he was smart enough not to spend everything that his master had trusted into his hands. In my case, however, I was spending over 20,000 thousand US dollars on needs and bills, thinking I had excuses. I could not get myself to save, talk less of multiplying. The Lord also reminded me that there was a time I was making only 2,000 US dollars in a month.

At that time I had prayed to God that He should increase me. My belief was that if God could only help me make 5,000 US dollars in a month, I would be grateful and that that would be more than enough for me. Guess what? God answered that prayer, but once we started making 5,000 US dollars, the needs were already overwhelming, so much that the amount was again not enough because I was not following the laws of money. When you don't abide by the laws of money and like in my case you don't even know them, it means that caterpillars and cankerworms are always standing by to consume the little that you make.

Here I was again rushing to God in prayer to increase our income to 10,000 US dollars. I was sure that if we could earn 10,000 US dollars we would never be in need again. Well, you can guess what happened. My rude awakening happened when we were already making 20,000 US dollars and yet not meeting our needs. God's conviction was so strong that I had no option but to break down in sorrow and repentance. The straw that broke the camel's back came when I said to the Lord, I know I am not lazy by any standard, but you spoke of that man as being lazy.

At that point, I was working 18 hours a day. How can I be working for 18 hours and still be called lazy? Again the Lord came to my rescue, He said by being lazy here, He was talking about my refusal to think, laziness of the mind in relation to money. He said the laws and the principles of managing money are out there; I should not have been so lazy not to go in search of them and my failure to develop myself in the question of finances was also a form of laziness.

The fact that I did not bother to study financial matters or even go for financial consultations all pointed in the direction of this laziness – mental laziness. I thought I had an excuse, my argument was I am a pastor, I want to do my business, besides I had never heard any pastor preach or teach on this. To which the Lord told me, that is not an excuse and I am answerable only to Him. He has all the knowledge for anyone that is diligent enough to ask, seek and knock.

This revelation changed my life for good. Immediately

after this, I called the board of our church and I declared to them that we were going to cut a lot of our expenses with a significant part of our income going on savings and eventually into investments. That was another hurdle that I needed to surmount, because my board said, we are a church, and we don't do investments, we only spend, we don't invest or multiply.

To cut the long story short, I was able to get the church to start putting aside the first ten percent of all that came in for savings and investments. We gradually moved from there to thirty percent of all that came in for savings and investments. As a result, I was able to make our church a millionaire church in one year, that is in surplus. After attaining this with the church, I dared to challenge myself to make my first million US dollars in the next two years. I studied all I could on the subject. With my experience from helping the church make money, I was surprised when after 9 months I was able to make my first million US dollars instead of in 2 years.

For my next target, I decided to prove the efficacy of these principles by helping my church members become millionaires. I started with ordinary people and by the grace of God in the next three years, I was able to raise 200 millionaires in US dollars from within our congregation. Yes, the die had been cast. The Lord was right after all. I had learned my lessons. No more going back!!!

I have come to discover a total of 25 Laws of money. All the laws and principles of making and multiplying money that I have learned over the years I put in my book called **"MONEY WON'T MAKE YOU RICH"** You can get a copy for yourself, you will be glad you did.

# CHAPTER 15
# GOLDEN POINTS

1. Universal laws don't segregate; whoever and wherever you are you can stop working for Uncle Sam through mastery of the universal laws of Money.

2. You need to understand that money is not a miracle; it must either be earned or created.

3. The right knowledge is the key; you are what you are today because of what you know or don't know.

4. Perfection is attained through fervent practice.

5. The knowledge you don't put to practice won't work for you.

6. On the journey for freedom from the dominion of Uncle Sam; you need to stop listening to the dictates of money.

7. You have overcome the grip of money don't allow it to control you rather be the one controlling money.

8. It is impossible to conduct an honest personality evaluation before going on to stop working for Uncle Sam.

9. Make people who patronize your workplace be indebted to you.

10. Don't eat your seed rather invest it; invest it by putting it in ventures that are tested as authentic methods of multiplying money.

## CHAPTER SIXTEEN

# HAVE TOO MUCH MONEY

*"How do I define success? Let me tell you, money's pretty nice. But having a lot of money does not automatically make you a successful person. What you want is money and meaning. You want your work to be meaningful, because meaning is what brings the real richness to your life."*
(Oprah Winfrey)

There are only two problems with money, either you have none or very little of it, or you have too much money. Many Christians want to downplay the importance of money to say we don't need too much of it. Unfortunately, Christians world over want to have money enough to only meet their family's day to day needs. In this book, you have by now learned that Christians should not work for money to just meet needs. The goal should be to become so financially wealthy that you can be a kingdom promoter.

Through their wealth, non-Christians have gone ahead to sponsor some very bad programs while Christians just sit by and watch. Issues of pornography have got big funders; people who are corrupting morals with their money. Christians should no longer be content with just having enough to meet daily needs. If you are going to stop working for Uncle Sam and forever live free from that bondage you need to have too much money.

Even though it is currently about 3% of people on earth who are in that bracket of commanding too much money, you too can join that clique through the diligent study, hard work and constant application of the laws of money.

## WHY SHOULD CHRISTIAN NEED TO HAVE TOO MUCH MONEY?

**"But thou shalt remember the LORD thy God: for it is he that giveth thee power to get wealth, that he may establish his covenant which he sware unto thy fathers, as it is this day"**

*Deuteronomy 8:18.*

The passage shows us a very important aspect of a Christian's wealth. The reason you need wealth is so that you can establish the kingdom of God. Christians need a lot of money not necessary for their own consumption but as faithful stewards to use it appropriately as the master deems fit.

You too my reader should aspire for great wealth. Wealth is for the purpose of establishing the kingdom of God on the earth. Without money, Christians will accomplish very little in this world. When King Solomon asked God for wisdom to govern Israel, God added riches to him because with wisdom you only have the ideas, methods, and plans of bringing solutions but money will create the platform to implement them. A lot of money should be the ideal for every Christian so that their concern will only be to propagate the kingdom of God.

In an early chapter, I introduced you to Manny

Pacquiao. I want to cite a few highlights from his life to illustrate to you the impact Millionaire Christians can have on society.

Legend Sugar Ray Leonard warned Pacquiao about being too generous with his earnings just before he fought with Mayweather in what was called the "Fight of the century". This warning just testifies that Manny is known by many people as a generous giver. Filipino boxing promoter Bob Arum also remarked that Pacquiao will no doubt give half of the proceeds from the fight to good causes. He said: "I'm sure half of what Manny earns in this fight is going to go to charity. That is just Manny". "The "Fight of the century" as it was advertised had crossed the 400 Million USD mark, showing just how much money was trooping in for this Mega fight.

After paying out the organizers and the media reps, the check was split between the two boxers 60-40 with Mayweather getting the lion's share. Records show that Pacquiao has earned approximately 25 to 30 Million USD per fight regularly in the past. This Champion for Christ has millions that are available to sponsor kingdom undertakings to the glory of God. Other boxers spend their fortune on gold, girls, cars and parties; Manny, on the other hand, uses the fortune to demonstrate the love of Jesus Christ.

Christian millionaires can do more for the kingdom than poor Christians can. As a result of his wealth, Manny was able to donate about $40 million to charity. This shows us that more money for Christian would translate into more kingdom impact. Why should Christians be millionaires? Christians can use their millions to reach and impact millions of souls with kingdom values.

## THE FALLACY THAT A LOT OF MONEY WILL CAUSE CHRISTIANS TO ABANDON THE FAITH

A life of hardship is neither necessary nor righteous thus being poor does not get you closer to God. And being rich does not hide God's face from an individual. For centuries the church had tried by all means to teach people that wealth was evil. Even today they're ministers who sternly warn their members against desiring wealth.

I do agree that *"the love of money is the root of all evil"*. The love of money is to be avoided but not the obtaining of a lot much money. You can have a lot much money and still not love money. This may be hard for some religious minds but that is just the plain truth.

The key to overcoming the love of money we have already discussed is making money your slave. If you are a master over money you don't need to worry about the love of money. *"If riches increase, set not your heart upon them" Psalms 62:10b*. If your priority is loving God, and seeking to establish His kingdom and righteousness on the earth then you will not be overcome by the love of money. To overcome the love of money you must place God at the center of your life. Then you won't worry about coming under the dominion of money no matter how much you acquire.

What causes Christians to compromise their faith when riches increase is that they put money first instead of lording over it. If God is the treasure of your heart then no matter how much money you acquire it will not bring you into compromise.

# THE TREASURE OF YOUR HEART

**"For where your treasure is, there will your heart be also"**

*Luke 12:34*

Make God the treasure of your heart and the increase of wealth will certainly remain a blessing. "Jesus said unto him, Thou shalt love the Lord thy God with all thy heart, and with all thy soul, and with all thy might". Your love defines the treasure of your heart. In our quest to have a lot of money the only care that should linger in our minds is "HOW" we can love our God and best express our love for him. Loving him should be the driving force even when you increase in wealth. Christians should use their wealth to express their love for God and who knows what that love can do for this world.

The Bible tells us in 1 John 4:20 that "If a man says, *"I love God," and hates his brother, he is a liar; for he who doesn't love his brother whom he has seen*, how can he love God whom he has not seen? Thus the evidence of your love for God is seen by how you love your fellow men. So when I say use your wealth to express your love for God, it is expressed by doing good towards your fellow men.

It is my firm belief that every Christian can and should become a millionaire for the expression of God's kingdom on the earth.

May your efforts in setting yourself free from Uncle Sam be greatly rewarded as you work towards having a lot of money!!!

# CHAPTER 16
# GOLDEN POINTS

1. The goal should be for every Christian to become so financially wealthy that they can be kingdom promoters.

2. You too can join that clique of wealth commanders through the diligent study, correct and constant application of the laws of money.

3. Wealth is for the purpose of establishing the kingdom of God on the earth.

4. Without money, Christians will accomplish very little in this world.

5. A lot of money should be the ideal for every Christian so that their concern will only be to propagate the kingdom of our God.

6. The key to overcoming the love of money is making money your slave.

# PART IV

## STOP WORKING FOR UNCLE SAM

## CHAPTER SEVENTEEN

# WHAT IT MEANS TO STOP WORKING FOR UNCLE SAM

As I draw this discourse towards a conclusion I want to emphasize various points that are cardinal in your quest to stop working for and live free from Uncle Sam. Firstly to stop working for Uncle Sam does not mean a cessation from all work. This book is no way a promotion of laziness but hard work. Work, as God designed not as dictated by Uncle Sam. To be a person of influence in the area of your passion demands hard work and discipline. Thus stopping for Uncle Sam means one turns his attention towards using his gift and talents to the glory of God.

### STOP WORKING FOR UNCLE SAM MEANS – FREEDOM TO OBEY THE LORD JESUS CHRIST ANYTIME

To stop working for Uncle Sam means you are free and able to obey the Lord Jesus Christ any time without worry about how you would survive because you already have money working for you. It means you have been able to create or set up a system whereby you will be able to live and do God's will and still be able to pay bills and meet life's necessities.

What makes Christians world over fail to live in obedience to the Lord's commands is that they are dependent on the worldly systems to meet their daily needs and as such bring themselves under enslavement.

To stop working for Uncle Sam therefore implies firstly the freedom to obey the Lord Jesus Christ and secondly the setting up of systems of financial flow to enable an appropriate response to any need of life.

## STOP WORKING FOR UNCLE SAM MEANS – WORK FOR YOURSELF AND MAKE MONEY TO WORK FOR YOU

To stop working for Uncle Sam stands for the journey of freedom to either working for yourself or have your money work for you. It is easy to make your hobbies your work when you are working for yourself. Usually, when you are working for another person you are subjected to their conditions. But when you stop working for Uncle Sam you become independent. You can make decisions that bring glory to God and make you happy. Remember the Job's morning question?

> *"I have looked in the mirror every morning and asked myself: "if today were the last day of my life, would I want to do what am about to do today?" And whenever the answer has been "No" for too many days in a row, I know I need to change something"*
> *(Steve Jobs)*

When you are working for yourself you can almost always answer in the affirmative the Steve Job's morning question. The idea is for you to do the work you were born to do as you work for yourself. Money and survival should not be the underlying motive behind your work. If your work is your passion and calling then you are truly free from Uncle Sam.

## STOP WORKING FOR UNCLE SAM MEANS – YOU ARE MANAGING AND CONTROLLING MONEY

Another meaning of you stopping to work for Uncle Sam is that you have money working for you and all you are doing is managing and controlling it. Directing money where to go and multiplying itself becomes your work. Having money work for you implies investments. One of the Laws of money states that'; *"any amount of money that comes to your hand must not be spent until a significant part of it is invested"*.

You are lazy if you spend all that comes to you. Failure to find ideas and ventures that can grow your money is laziness. That spending of all income is a signal of Uncle Sam's dominion. Thus to stop working for Uncle Sam means you have various investment portfolios that are making money for you even when you are sleeping. That is the purpose of temporarily working for Uncle Sam system; to raise the capital you can later invest. To stop working for Uncle Sam means therefore that you have money multiplying itself and it sponsors your kingdom enterprises.

## STOP WORKING FOR UNCLE SAM MEANS – YOU HAVE DISCOVERED YOUR PASSION AND ENGAGING IN IT

To stop working for Uncle Sam system means you have discovered what your calling is and you are working there. It is the place or work, where you find satisfaction and it is something that flows out of you naturally. You cannot claim to be free from Uncle Sam if what you are doing is not the passion and calling of your life. If your work is not your prime calling it means therefore that the work you are doing is just for salary and survival. And you are still working for Uncle Sam. To stop working for Uncle Sam entails that passion has become the motivation behind your work. Freedom from the bondage of Uncle Sam is freedom to do the work you love.

## STOP WORKING FOR UNCLE SAM MEANS - GETTING OUT OF ANY SYSTEM HOLDING YOU IN BONDAGE

To stop working for Uncle Sam system means to get out of any system that is holding you in bondage. Why are you failing to speak out for the cause of the kingdom? You have to get tired of constantly being under the command of people who may not even appreciate the work you do. If you are working in a place where you are continually being castigated, reprimanded and being threatened with sack speeches, you are in bondage. Get out of that system. Plan and work hard to get out of that bondage. You are under restrictions every now and then, answering charges always because you are in bondage. Stop working for Uncle Sam implies you breaking free from that bondage to serve your God wholeheartedly.

## STOP WORKING FOR UNCLE SAM MEANS – GET OUT OF THE SYSTEM MAKING YOU NOT TO BE YOURSELF

To stop working for Uncle Sam means you getting out of any system that is making you not to be yourself. Men pleasures are some of the frustrated masses on planet earth. You can't keep living your life for others. When you are constantly under pressure to please your employer, you are under captivity. Many pretenders are found in Uncle Sam system; pretending to be enjoying work meanwhile they detest it. They pretend to like their boss but in truth the find his presence unbearable.

Working for Uncle Sam many times entails suppressing one's true self. To stop working for Uncle Sam means you are working without the pressure of pleasing any man. Your work should enable you to express your true self thereby giving you the opportunity to work with plea-sure.

It is better for a person to do work that brings them true self-expression than that which pays them hand-somely. If you remain faithful to the work of your passion you will for sure find happiness, fulfillment and mone-tary rewards too. Stop working for Uncle Sam; get out of any system that is making you not to be yourself.

## STOP WORKING FOR UNCLE SAM MEANS – GETTING OUT OF ANY SYSTEM THAT IS MAKING YOU DEPENDENT ON IT

To stop working for Uncle Sam system means to get out of any system that makes you be dependent on it. If you can't leave your work to obey God, it means you are still under the bondage of Uncle Sam. Whatever system that has you captivated such that you have to keep working for survival is your Uncle Sam. Leave that system that makes you feel that you are done for without it. The system that brings a feeling of fear of survival and failure to meet daily needs is Uncle Sam and you need to determine to leave at all cost. Leave the system; be free to serve your God in the work of your passion and calling.

## YOU MUST OUTSMART THE SYSTEM

After having read this book you just can't afford to continue working for Uncle Sam anymore. You are a person of great potentials and abilities that you can employ to the glory of God and the expansion of his Kingdom. The only thing you need is a strong resolve to stop working for Uncle Sam. This worldly system has captivated millions under its bondage but you can out-smart the system and escape the traps that are set on the way.

There is no great joy than being a kingdom dispenser. Work is a means through you can use to flood the earth with God's glory. Men yearn to see God and we have been sent to reveal his nature and love to the people of the world. True satisfaction is only attained when we focus on bringing the kingdom of God to our various professions.

There are decisions to make, steps to take to come to the place of freedom from Uncle Sam's dominion. Christians should work to set up enterprises that stand for Godly justice and founded on truth. When Christians stop working for Uncle Sam the earth will be filled with the glory of our God. Jesus showed us that our priority in prayer should be the request of the manifestation of the Kingdom of God. If the kingdom is our priority in prayer then it also needs to be our priority in our work and various professions.

A lot of Christians can bring the kingdom of God

to this earth if only they had the money. We as Christians are not to be afraid of having a lot of money. The purpose of money must be to advance the kingdom of our God. Stop working for Uncle Sam and get busy doing kingdom business by engaging your passion and talents. Many believers have been conditioned to see themselves as underachievers who cannot amount to anything. The correct attitude and mindset is that every Christian can and should become a millionaire; commanding serious wealth for the expansion of the Kingdom. My desire is to see the Church of Christ rise to go beyond the closed four walls of the church and begin to take over the world. Christians can make a mark for God on the earth if only they stop spending their lives working for Uncle Sam.

The time to gain mastery over money is now; you must break free from being a slave of money. You don't have to work for money all your life, there is something better and greater you can do with your life. You are created for a special mission and it is not to work for and retire in Uncle Sam's system. The dependence on Uncle Sam proves that God is not your master. If Christ is your Lord, you will break free from Uncle Sam system to serve him all the time, anytime. This book is an effort to get you to wake up and realize who you are working for in your regular job.

When you succumb to the pressure of getting a regular job for a regular salary you are working for Uncle Sam. Salary is a serious undervaluation of the great potentials, gifts, and calling of your life. Refuse to give in to the pressure of everyday life of survival, simply making money to meet needs. STOP WORKING FOR UNCLE SAM!

# EPILOGUE – TAKE ACTION

*Successful seems to be connected with action. Successful people keep moving. They make mistakes but they don't quit"*

(Conrad Hilton)

Beloved, **"Saying 'I want to save 20%' doesn't mean anything. You should be clear and precise; why do you want to save money?"**

For example, you can decide to put yourself on a one-year shopping ban. Do you realize that it's harder for most people to skip their morning coffee just for the sake of having $500 more in the bank every year? Rather, think about that $500 as a short-term sacrifice in the name of a long-term goal. The action you take may start with small steps but in the long run, those small steps will pay off.

I want to admonish you once again with several reminders about your need to take action.

**"And there were four leprous men at the entering in of the gate: and they said one to another, why sit we here until we die?"**

2 Kings 7:3.

Indecision is also a decision. Just sitting and hoping will not work for you in your quest for liberty from Uncle Sam. Decide now to start looking for ways and means to set yourself free from the dominion and lordship of Uncle Sam. Means are created were a strong desire for change exists. That decision must be taken, if you don't take the decision and just wait for the opportunity, the opportunity will not come.

> **"I returned, and saw under the sun, that the race is not to the swift, nor the battle to the strong, neither yet bread to the wise, nor yet riches to men of understanding, nor yet favour to men of skill; but time and chance happeneth to them all"**
>
> *Ecclesiastes 9:11*

Chance will only favor those who are prepared. If you refuse to prepare yourself through learning and practicing the laws of money you won't manage to free yourself from Uncle Sam's dominion. The above passage gives us the assurance that life has no favorites. If you prepare, you will explore the chances of life. Resolve today to begin working towards your freedom.

Don't just sit and wait for a miracle, take the step. If you take that decision, God will bless that it and you will vividly see your progression out of Uncle Sam's domineering hand.

If you sit you die, it is time to make the decision and take that step. It was not until the four lepers moved that a miracle happened. The step you take towards a hopeful future is what actuates the miracle in your life. God will not do for you what He has told and equipped you to do. The power and thunder of the almighty will be the sound of the human steps you make towards freedom. The four lepers were faced with several choices and they took the most risky but promising and profitable choice. Don't let fear incapacitate your mobility. Many people don't want to pay the price for the life they aspire for. They say *"a journey of a thousand miles begins with a step"*. For sure even the journey to a life free from Uncle Sam will not happen overnight but every single step taken is very significant and should not be despised. Move and God will bless your effort.

A popular Japanese proverb says, *"Vision without action is a daydream. Action without vision is a nightmare"*. Having a vision is equally important as taking action. These two aspects must be combined to get the success mix.

I recently came across the story of Mark and Britney Johnston who in just 2 years were able to save $40,000. *"We realized we didn't have to go extremes for this. At first, we were intimidated by cutting expenses and living really frugally, but it wasn't that bad."* This saving enabled them to follow their passion and they could travel the world. The lump sum of $40,000 sounds like a lot, but once they broke it down into $1,000 a month each, they realized it was much easier than they thought. The strategy of breaking down the huge goal into smaller achievable milestones was the motivation they needed. That's the strategy you can devise.

You can plan to work in Uncle Sam for a few years, 5 years as maximum proposed early. That's 60 months of small steps that will culminate into the dream of stopping to work for Uncle Sam. If you plan to save $1,000 like the Johnstons you will be able to save $60,000 to invest. If you are a couple and both receiving an income, you can propose to each save a $500 monthly for the 5 years that would afford you the chance of avoiding very drastic cut downs.

It is time to get your plan in order for an assured exit out of Uncle Sam system. Today is the day for action tomorrow is not promised. If you can't do it today what makes you confident that you will do it tomorrow? Don't delay the action you know you must do. Postponement of action is an invariably postponement of the result. As long as you keep pushing that decision for-ward you are also delaying the result and benefits attached to it.

God will bless the action you take but if you are just ending up in a plan, you are still far. You can have the right plan but it is of no use only as a plan it must be backed by action steps. So develop a plan and assign action; that's what is called an **"ACTION PLAN"**. Plan to take the step and then take it.

> *"Failing to plan is planning to fail"*
> *(Alan Lakein)*

# CONCLUSION:
# 30 POINT SUMMARY

1. Uncle Sam stands for the system of government that dominates and oppresses people.

2. Uncle Sam stands for the scenario when people have to be at the mercy of government, sell their liberties, sell their freedom and government pays them a salary in return. The people have to give their whole life just to have some money for survival.

3. In modern ideology, the term Uncle Sam stands for any kind of dependence on any system or organization that makes you look up to that organization, company or individual for employment to earn some money for survival.

4. Working for Uncle Sam goes beyond exploitation, in a broader sense, it is a system of bondage whereby you are living in a society that controls you. A system where you have to pay bills and look continually for how you can make a living.

5. Uncle Sam is any job that ties you down and deprives you of your will and freedom.

6. Your salary disappears faster than you succeed in receiving the next. You work but at the end of the day, you don't see where your income goes to then you are working for Uncle Sam.

7. When you are working for Uncle Sam, The system decides what happens to your income rather than you making the decisions. The

expenditure of your income is planned and spent for you by the system almost up to 50%.

8. Uncle Sam is a vicious cycle which once you get into only spits your out when all the juice of your working productive life is spent.

9. Uncle Sam symbolizes a life of illusion, i.e. the 'American Dream'. You are encouraged to work hard, study hard for you to become what you want to be.

10. Do a careful examination of your life; how can you account for the past ten, fifteen or twenty years of your life. What tangible things can you point to even though you have been working?

11. It is through desire for money that Uncle Sam uses to enslave people.

12. You are either a master over or a slave to money

13. The Uncle Sam system keeps people working all their lives without teaching them the Laws of money

14. Uncle Sam is structured in a way that the only thing it teaches you is how to spend money.

15. Due to our desire to make more money and provide better living conditions for our families, we become slaves to our jobs.

16. We need to master money and dominate it so that we can use it to serve God in our given purpose.

17. The idea of work in God's economy is not for survival but to fulfill purpose.

18. If you are working for survival then you are a slave to Uncle Sam

19. Christians should not work for money but for their calling and purpose

20. For you to truly be free to serve your God and to fulfill the purpose for which he sent you here on earth you must do everything you need to do to set yourself free from the bondage of Uncle Sam.

21. To stop working for Uncle Sam you must discover your passion and calling.

22. Know and perfect the laws of money

23. The goal to stop working for Uncle Sam should be to have too much money.

24. Christians should go to work with only one purpose in mind; to bring the kingdom of God in that sphere of life God has called them to.

25. If we are going to work only to make a living or survive it means we are not serving God in and through our work but we are using our work to serve Uncle Sam.

26. Matthew 6:33; Kingdom citizens must not be motivated by survival but by purpose.

27. The first purpose of your Job and employment should be to bring the kingdom of God to bare and rule in your workplace not to get a salary.

28. Our salary, paychecks and job promotions are therefore God's way of rewarding our faithfulness in seeking his kingdom first.

29. For a Christian, work should be a way to serve God, a way of establishing His kingdom on earth.

30. All work, therefore, must be to serve God, and money must only be seen as a byproduct of such service.

*FOR THE LOVE OF GOD, CHURCH, AND NATION*
*By Pastor Sunday Adelaja*

## REFERENCES

1. Rich Dad Poor Dad: What the rich teach their kids about money that the poor and middle class don't – page 1
2. http://www.excellerate.co.nz/blog/why_we_stay_in_jobs_we_hate.html
3. http://www.businessinsider.com/6-stories-of-job-loss-that-will-inspire-2013-7
4. http://www.cato.org/publications/commentary/how-big-brother-began
5. https://www.theguardian.com/business/2014/mar/19/orange-france-investigates-second-wave-suicides
6. http://www.healthline.com/health-news/baby-boomer-suicide-rate-rising-031515#9
7. http://www.history.com/this-day-in-history/united-states-nicknamed-uncle-sam
8. http://americanhistory.si.edu/blog/2013/09/uncle-sam-the-man-and-the-meme-the-origins-of-uncle-sam.html
9. http://unitedvoicesmedia.com/pdfs/WORLDCLASS-SUPPERSTARMESSI.pdf
10. http://www.history-of-soccer.org/lionel-messi-biography.html
11. http://americanhistory.si.edu/sites/default/files/blog_files/a/6a00e553a80e108834019aff524784970c-800wi.png
12. Consumer's guide to Repossession Practices (Bureau of Security and Investigative Services, www.bsis.ca.gov)
13. http://www.forbes.com/pictures/eimh45ehjl/steve-jobs-live-each-day-as-if-it-was-your-last/#5ebbcdfd6287
14. http://www.bls.gov/news.release/empsit.nr0.htm
15. World employment and social outlook: Trends 2015 / International Labour Office. – Geneva: ILO, 2015. Page 19
16. http://www.healthline.com/health-news/baby-boomer-suicide-rate-rising-031515#9, Accessed 28.07.2016

17. http://www.cbsnews.com/htdocs/pdf/poll_050409americandream.pdf
18. http://theconversation.com/is-the-american-dream-dead-57095
19. Bruce Barton, 1930
20. Suze Orman: https://www.youtube.com/watch?v=lCn-oVu1z4qc
21. Social Security vs. Private Retirement, Pro. Antony Davies: https://www.youtube.com/watch?v=PLTfOAY-fbao
22. http://www.heritage.org/research/reports/2015/09/poverty-and-the-social-welfare-state-in-the-united-states-and-other-nations
23. http://www.healthline.com/health-news/baby-boomer-suicide-rate-rising-031515#9
24. http://www.forbes.com/sites/brettowens/2015/12/19/2-reits-profiting-from-baby-boomers-ventas-and-welltower/#709f687f6e1a
25. http://www.forbes.com/2008/12/12/madoff-ponzi-hedge-pf-ii-in_rl_1212croesus_inl.html
26. Ponzi scheme: Concise Oxford English Dictionary
27. Slave: Concise Oxford English Dictionary
28. Master: Concise Oxford English Dictionary
29. Education: Concise Oxford English Dictionary
30. http://www.forbes.com/sites/laurengensler/2016/05/27/couple-saves-one-million-early-retirement-travel/#-62133fad47f8
31. http://www.worldbank.org/projects/P130459/development-policy-loan-2?lang=en
32. Young Chinese feeling trapped by pressure to marry: http://www.globaltimes.cn/content/968204.shtml
33. If this cow dies, we all die. Kit Flowers: http://www.ccel.us/alifewelllived.ch12.html
34. http://www.historymakers.info/inspirational-christians/jim-elliot.html

35. http://www.brainyquote.com/quotes/quotes/j/jimel-liot189244.html
36. Jim Elliot. BrainyQuote.com, Xplore Inc, 2016.
37. http://www.forbes.com/sites/jacque-lynsmith/2013/10/07/six-tips-for-turning-your-hobby-into-your-job/#6042585a1e85
38. http://www.cbsnews.com/news/oregon-judge-vance-day-refuses-perform-same-sex-marriages-religious-grounds/
39. http://www.brainyquote.com/quotes/quotes/j/jimel-liot189244.html, accessed July 29, 2016.
40. http://www.transamericacenter.org/docs/default-source/global-survey-2016/tcrs2016_i_life-events.pdf
41. http://www.transamericacenter.org/docs/default-source/global-survey-2016/tcrs2016_pr_retirement_wake_up_call.pdf
42. http://christianpf.com/what-to-do-when-you-hate-your-job/
43. https://www.transamericacenter.org/docs/default-source/global-survey-2015/tcrs2016_cr_flexible_retire-ment_in_us.pdf
44. https://www.transamericacenter.org/docs/default-source/global-survey-2015/tcrs2016_cr_flexible_retire-ment_in_cn.pdf
45. https://www.whywork.org/about/faq/wageslave.html
46. http://www.ccel.us/alifewelllived.ch9.html
47. http://thecrux.com/must-read-how-to-stop-being-a-slave-and-start-living-life-on-your-own-terms/
48. Harvard Business Review: https://hbr.org/2011/05/the-power-of-small-wins
49. http://www.telegraph.co.uk/sport/othersports/boxing/manny-pacquiao/11563214/Manny-Pacquiao-24-things-you-didnt-know.html
50. https://www.kalibrr.com/advice/2015/05/manny-pac-quiao-success-story-willl-inspire-you/

51. https://www.theguardian.com/sport/2014/oct/04/manny-pacquiao-chris-algieri-floyd-mayweather

52. http://www.express.co.uk/sport/boxing/574203/Manny-Pacquiao-donate-Mayweather-fight-earning-charity

53. http://www.carmudi.pk/journal/manny-pacquiao-donates-half-his-paycheck-to-charity/

54. Dr. Myles Munroe: Kingdom principals – Preparing for kingdom experience and Expansion, Page 25, 82.

55. http://anonhq.com/true-reason-behind-40-hour-work-week-economic-slaves/

56. http://www.forbes.com/sites/jacquelynsmith/2013/10/07/six-tips-for-turning-your-hobby-into-your-job/#6042585a1e85

57. http://bleacherreport.com/articles/209730-faith-in-sports-a-list-influential-christians-in-the-sports-world

58. David Oyedepo: Exploring the Secrets of Success

59. http://www.cbsnews.com/news/oregon-judge-vance-day-refuses-perform-same-sex-marriages-religious-grounds/

60. HTTP://WWW.PUJOLSFAMILYFOUNDATION.ORG/DISCOVER/FAITH/

61. Catholic Online http://www.catholic.org/clife/teresa/, Accessed 30.07.2016

62. http://www.christiancareercenter.com/advice-and-resources/career-and-calling-articles/looking-for-a-calling-not-just-a-job

63. http://www1.cbn.com/movies/the-unlikely-success-of-tyler-perry, Accessed 10.08.2016

64. http://www.biography.com/people/tyler-perry-361274#synopsis, Accessed 10.08.2016

65. http://www.forbes.com/sites/laurengensler/2015/12/02/superstar-savers-words-of-wisdom-from-ordinary-people-with-extaordinary-savings/#2673ce2234e8

# Sunday Adelaja Biography

Sunday Adelaja is a Nigerian born Leader, Transformation Strategist, Pastor, and Innovator.

At 19, he won a scholarship to study in the former Soviet Union. He completed his master's program in Belorussia State University with distinction in journalism.

At 33, he had built the largest evangelical church in Europe; The Embassy of the Blessed Kingdom of God for All Nations.

Sunday Adelaja is one of the few individuals in our world who has been privileged to speak in the United Nations, Israeli Parliament, Japanese Parliament, and United States Senate.

The movement he pioneered has been instrumental in reshaping lives of people in the Ukraine, Russia and about 50 other nations where he has his branches.

His congregation, which consists of ninety-nine percent white Europeans, is a cross-cultural model of the church for the 21st century.

His life mission is to advance the Kingdom of God on earth by raising a generation of history makers who will live for a cause larger, bigger, and greater than themselves. Those who will live like Jesus and transform every sphere of the society in every nation as a model of the Kingdom of God on earth.

His economic empowerment program has succeeded in raising over 200 millionaires in the short period of three years.

Sunday Adelaja is the author of over 300 books; many of which are translated into several languages including Russian, English, French, Chinese, German, etc.

His work has been widely reported by world media outlets such as; The Washington Post, The Wall Street Journal, New York Times, Forbes, Associated Press, Reuters, CNN, BBC, German, Dutch and French national television stations.

Pastor Sunday is happily married to his "Princess" Bose Dere Adelaja. They are blessed with three children; Perez, Zoe and Pearl.

# Follow Sunday Adelaja On Social Media

**Subscribe And Read Pastor Sunday's Blog:**

www.sundayadelajablog.com

**Follow These Links And Listen To Over 200 Of Pastor Sunday's Messages Free Of Charge:**

http://sundayadelajablog.com/content/

**Follow Pastor Sunday on Twitter:**

www.twitter.com/official_pastor

**Join Pastor Sunday's Facebook page to stay in touch:**

www.facebook.com/pastor.sunday.adelaja

**Visit our websites for more information about Pastor Sunday's ministry:**

http://www.godembassy.com
http://www.pastorsunday.com
http://sundayadelaja.de

# Contact

For distribution or to order bulk copies of
this book,
please contact us:

**USA**
CORNERSTONE PUBLISHING
info@thecornerstonepublishers.com
+1 (516) 547-4999
www.thecornerstonepublishers.com

**AFRICA**
Sunday Adelaja Media Ltd.
Email: btawolana@hotmail.com
+2348187518530, +2348097721451,
+2348034093699.

**LONDON, UK**
Pastor Abraham Great
abrahamagreat@gmail.com
+447711399828, +44-1908538141

**KIEV, UKRAINE**
pa@godembassy.org
Mobile: +380674401958

# Best Selling Books by Dr. Sunday Adelaja

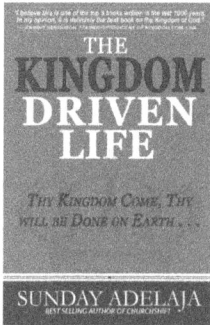

The Kingdom Driven Life:
Thy Kingdom Come, Thy
Will be Done on Earth
(Best seller)

Myles Munroe:
... Finding Answers To Why Good
People Die Tragic And Early Deaths

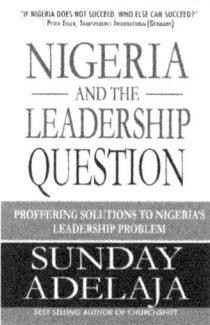

Nigeria And
The Leadership Question:
Proffering Solutions To Nige-
ria's Leadership Problem

Olorunwa (There Is Sunday):
Portrait Of Sunday Adelaja.
The Roads Of Life.

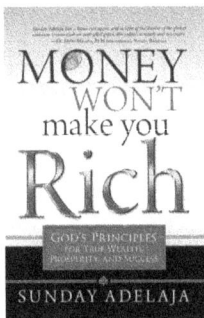

Money Won't Make You Rich:
God's Principles for True
Wealth, Prosperity, and Success

Who Am I? Why Am I here?:
How to discover your
purpose and calling in life

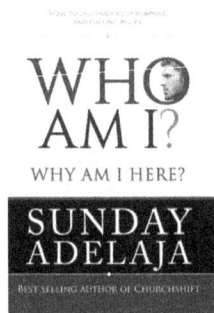

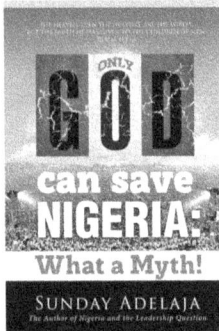

Only God Can Save Nigeria:
What a Myth?

Church Shift:
Revolutionizing Your Faith, Church,
and Life for the 21st Century

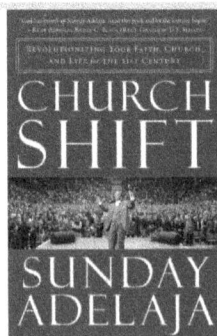

... and many more.

www.ingramcontent.com/pod-product-compliance
Lightning Source LLC
Chambersburg PA
CBHW031920190326
41519CB00007B/365